THE
REVEALING
EYE

THE REVEALING EYE

PERSONALITIES OF

THE 1920'S

IN PHOTOGRAPHS BY

NICKOLAS MURAY

AND WORDS BY

PAUL GALLICO

ATHENEUM

NEW YORK

1967

ACKNOWLEDGMENTS

We wish to thank Daniel W. Jones and Americo Giannicchi—friends, colleagues, artists—whose advice and assistance in preparing the photographs for publication were invaluable.

This book could not have been realized without the selfless devotion of Peggy Muray in carrying out the project which had just been begun by her late husband, Nickolas Muray, at the time of his death and which was very close to his heart—the presentation of the best of his work in portraiture. PAUL GALLICO

THE REVEALING EYE

NOTHING arouses the curiosity of human beings more than other human beings. Gossip and tales are one facet, but when we hear stories about the famous of past generations, most of all we want to know what they looked like—to gather from their lineaments, the expression of their eyes, the set of their chins, or the telltale mouths, hints as to the kind of people they really were.

The child, turning the pages of his history book to study the lessons of what was done in the past, pauses over the illustrations of the doers for some additional clues as to why and how it was done.

They are restricted to stiff paintings and prints, the distillation of what the artist saw, softened by the political necessities of rendering the illusion of the magnetic mien of majesty, or the conferring of nobility and beauty upon features that were considerably lacking. Kings, queens, bishops, soldiers, statesmen are seen propped up, posed and painted like marionettes. The likenesses are possibly faithful, but what of the men and women behind them?

The starknesses of bygone wars, too, were confined to the painter's palette, canvas and eye. Sometimes when seen by such a one as Goya, they were as cruel and horrifying as the original, yet always tinctured by the imagination of the creator. One recalls the great canvases of the nineteenth century depicting Napoleonic battles: men, horses, cannon in furious, wild-eyed action, the dead and the dying. Yet, for all of the bloodstained bandages and drama, they evoke the feeling that it is the artist's arrangement and composition, and that somehow, in spite of the hacked corpses littering the ground, romance and glory have managed to creep into the representation. The living and the dead are heroes.

It was not until the invention of photography, and the development of the photographer's art by such early photographer–war-correspondents as Mathew Brady, that noncombatants for the first time saw what Armageddon, the soldier's death, filth and fatigue were really like. Through the photographs of the tired, tatterdemalion Civil Warriors of the 1860's in America—privates and generals alike in dirty, unkempt uniforms, the strain showing upon their unshaven faces and in the weary, lackluster gaze they turned to the uncompromising and revealing glass eye of the camera that Brady focused upon them—we saw truth.

As well, through the new art of camera portraiture and its refinements from the days of the first Daguerreotypes people were being presented and preserved for posterity as they really had been in life. For, while composition, posing and lighting all had their place, artist photographers were appearing upon the scene who were able to do more than merely reproduce the surfaces of human beings upon film or glass plates. Themselves sensitive and passionately interested in the mystery of living persons, they penetrated that façade put up by the sitter, studied the wonderful individuality

V

concealed by flesh and bone, and clicked their shutters upon the one electric fraction of a second of revelation.

An example of such revelation is contained in the study of the eighty-six-year-old Claude Monet made by Nickolas Muray in 1926, when he went to Giverney, outside Paris, on an assignment for *Vanity Fair* to capture some ten of the most renowned European creative personalities of the time.

Papa Monet was then ill and tired—he was not to live out the year—and unwilling to pose, but finally consented. Muray set to work quickly, and after a bit Monet asked, "*Eh bien*, my friend, and when are you going to start taking the pictures?"

Respectfully Muray replied, "But I have already taken half a dozen, *Maître*."

"But this is impossible!" declared the great Impressionist. "You haven't told me what to do, or where to look, and besides, there hasn't been any click."

Muray explained that he had a "silent shutter" and showed him the bulb he had been holding behind his back which, when pressed, opened and closed the aperture in a fifth-of-a-second exposure.

Monet roared with laughter and said, "That's a great trick indeed! So now you will know me as I am and not as I would have tried to hide myself from you."

As a result, all of the power, the majesty, the beauty and the manhood of Monet shine through the portrait in this volume.

But how truly the old gentleman spoke for all sitters past, present and future: "So now you will know me as I am and not as I would have tried to hide myself from you." For every person who is lured into the studio of the portraitist, for whatever purpose, presents a problem, provided the photographer is honest and not a studio hack who, through devious lighting and even more questionable retouching, achieves the same prettied-up effect as did the royal painters.

To begin with, individuals carry about with them an image, a mental picture of themselves, which more often than not is nothing at all like what they are. They are conscious of having a good side and a bad side in profile, and there is always something they have to conceal, whether it be poor teeth, a weak chin, the first faint signs of the approaching wattles of age or, if not physical defects, then faults of character—treachery, dishonesty, mendacity, greed or vanity—which their expressions often cannot hide. Their mirrors deceive them, and they in turn wish to lie to the camera. Besides which, there is the universal tendency to freeze up before the apparatus and present an attitude as stiff and rigid as a ventriloquist's dummy with the same set, toothy grin. The photographer must first be able to recognize the true personality of his visitor and then capture it.

Future generations will learn about us from moving pictures and television tapes as well—too much so, in fact. For the television camera has turned out to be the most monstrous Peeping Tom of all time, with the capacity, apparently, to peer directly into our innermost recesses and expose every little meanness, pomposity and falseness to such a point that many politicians tremble and certain of them refuse to subject themselves to it in debate. But for thoughtful intimacy and a relaxed and truthful version of the celebrity, the portrait study by the artist-photographer must continue to be supreme. He, more than any other type of reproducer in the rapid-fire, journalistic, picture-magazine world of today, must capture not merely individuals but whole segments of an era with his lens. For many of the sitters who pass through his studio or are hunted down by him in their lairs are important and historic figures.

How did they look? How did they dress? And, above all, what were they really like in their lives and times? The answers to these questions have been and still continue to be supplied by men of the caliber of Steichen, Karsh, Beaton, Baron and Muray.

The success of the *Daily News*, New York's greatest tabloid, was originally founded upon the use of pictures. True, for the most part they were dramatic action caught by highly competitive press photographers—fire, flood, earthquake, war, railroad and highway disasters, cyclones, etc. But there was also one hard and fast rule laid down by Captain Joseph Medill Patterson, who conceived the picture paper, and this was that every news story of a length of three paragraphs or over, in which a prominent name was mentioned, must if possible be illuminated by the face of the person mentioned.

Picture-stealing on the part of reporters became almost as important as picture-taking by the photographers. Love, marriage, divorce, scandal, tragedy—the face was the important thing. What did John Doe, who had just beaten in his wife's head with a hammer, look like? If it was a good rich Long Island murder, this physiognomy might be blown up to the proportions of the entire front or back page. If it was a cheapy, just off the Bowery, he would rate no more than a half-column cut. You could see them as well as read about them, and it bore out the axiom that one picture was worth a thousand words. The difference between the flashlight photo of the startled prisoner or the stolen vacation snapshot of the murdered girl and that of the portraitist is only one of refinement; it is the revelation—the seeing—that counts.

Purely as a by-product, the portraitist photographer registers contemporary fashion and couture, just as generations of painters have provided us with a full record of changing style down through the centuries. Here are the Twenties and the clothes of the Twenties, which, while they may not seem to have altered appreciably in the last half-century, have certainly changed radically from those of fifty years prior. Men still wear essentially the same attire—trousers and jacket. Women, while experimenting with trouser suits and the mini-skirt, by and large the world over still wear skirts, blouses, sweaters and frocks. Yet the clothing in these photographs is distinctively of the 1920's, as are the hair-dos of both men and women. Fifty years from now, we of today will appear as the sartorial prisoners of our own contemporary era, but with the aid of the photograph, anthropologists and students of dress will be able to study and comment upon development or retrogression year by year.

It is an astonishing fact that there are changing fashions in looks as well as in clothes. The girls of the Twenties seemed to run to full, rounded faces, square-jawed, into which were set a pair of large round eyes and a ridiculously small cupid's-bow mouth. The bobbed hair that went with this face added a curious kind of childish petulance to the expression. They were strangely sexless, at least seen through modern eyes, and if the screen actress known as Theda Bara, who was the sex symbol of the early days of the movies, were to appear today in the make-up she affected to depict

VII

passion, she would be greeted with roars of laughter.

The sex symbols have altered. In those times the word "voluptuous" was not yet considered ludicrous. Curves, hips and substantial bottoms were in. And if you will look at a Mack Sennett "still" of a slapstick harem comedy, or even an abstract of a serious scene set in a seraglio, you will see from the shapes and heft of the girls he hired that they were just what the Pasha ordered.

The latter-day sirens of stage and screen, and particularly the models that set the styles of sexual attraction supposed to rouse the often reluctant beast in the tired businessman, are lean-jawed, starvation-slender, big-eyed creatures typified by Audrey Hepburn, Jean Shrimpton or Twiggy. There are still some big-bosomed girls about, priestesses of the lingering remnants of the great American mammary cult. But compare the stars of stage, screen and advertising pages of yesterday and today and they seem almost to be creatures of different planets.

The men of that period managed to look prissy in their photographs, with too smooth skin and pretty profiles. Many of them parted their hair in the middle or sported what appeared to be a permanent wave, and the high, stiff collar that was de rigueur was of no aid to their image. Their heads sat perched upon these like Easter eggs. Dressed in the street clothes of the period, they appear to us today as asexual and prim as their female counterparts of stage and screen, and one wonders how they ever managed to get together. Yet the fact remains that they did. And in the plays and the movies, the operas and the ballets that were drawing huge audiences into the theaters, they managed even to generate considerable voltage.

Yet, unpretty as the post-World War I styles look to us today, their wearers were actually in the throes of the first great American emancipatory renaissance, a good deal of which seemed to be characterized by the title of a popular song that went the rounds shortly after the last of the returning doughboys from abroad had been unloaded: "How Ya Gonna Keep 'Em Down on the Farm, After They've Seen Paree?"

Post-World War I saw the first loosening of the bonds of the Victorian strait jacket which had restrained practically all classes of Americans for close to half a century. The American inheritance of prudery was even more severe than that of the British, and when we began to fling off restraint, we flang high, wide and handsome.

It was, of course, nothing to compare with the total abandonment of standards of morality, conduct, speech and license following some twenty years after World War II, in which we find ourselves wallowing today. But for a starter it wasn't bad, combined as it was with the well-nigh incredible orgy of drunkenness and lawlessness inspired by Prohibition.

But it was not only a period of license following upon restraint; it was far more a time of emancipation from outworn and outmoded ideas, and an evolution. The arts flourished. The men and women in this book were the principal participants in a vast cultural revolution.

People of the theater were no longer considered infra-dig and arose from the low esteem in which actors and actresses had been held throughout the previous century to become national idols, not only through the elevation of the stage and the improving quality of public taste in plays, but through the medium of motion pictures as well. Not only were show people idolized, but for the first time millions of Americans began to live actors' lives via "fan" magazines, taking them vicariously into their homes, where, like the sports heroes of the times, they became members of the family.

Radio and newspaper publicity helped to disseminate information about these rising stars. But in many ways it seemed as though America had grown up almost overnight and made the transition from the rough-and-tumble, self-conscious people of the middle and late nineteenth century to appreciation, discrimination and sophistication. The great boom that began in the Twenties brought about those conditions that are always basic to any sudden cultural leap forward—peace, money and leisure.

It is difficult to realize that only a little more than a hundred years ago one of the world's great singers, the soprano Jenny Lind, known as the "Swedish Nightingale," was sponsored and presented on her only American tour by a circus impresario, Phineas T. Barnum, who regarded her as a freak to be exploited because of her fame in Europe, rather than as an artist with the most glorious voice of her times.

Prints of Whistler's mother and Reynolds' *Innocence* were the only reproductions hung in American homes, and as late as 1917 there was a terrific to-do over a French painting of a nude girl, known as *September Morn*. Yet it was just a decade later that Nickolas Muray was assigned to go abroad to photograph the French Impressionist Claude Monet. Scales were beginning to fall from American eyes, and not only paintings were becoming important, but the men and women who painted them as well. Through the medium of such magazines as *Vanity Fair* and *Harper's Bazaar*, Americans became aware of home-grown artists, musicians, playwrights, sculptors such as George Bellows, George Gershwin, Mischa Elman, Jascha Heifetz, Paul Manship, Willa Cather, Edna Ferber, Ralph Barton and others, as well as the Europeans of the caliber of Shaw, H. G. Wells, Hall Caine, D. H. Lawrence, Monet, Andrés Segovia, Chaliapin, Bartók, Gertrude Lawrence, Nazimova and Yvette Guilbert, who were beginning to have a strong impact upon American art, life and letters.

It is a curious fact that, thinking and writing of the Twenties today, one tends to forget that this was the decade of the very worst manifestations of the Prohibition law, and that much of the excitement and melodrama of the period was furnished by the daily serial of cops and robbers, or rather bootleggers and Prohibition agents, with a marvelous obbligato of Crime-on-the-House, the exciting internecine warfare of the gangsters who provided the country's drinking lawbreakers with alcohol.

For the first time murder lost some of its shock value and even took on an aspect of entertainment. We were all placed in the enviable position of the man watching his mother-in-law fighting a bear and not really caring who won. The liquor purveyors eliminated one another most engagingly with pistols, shotguns, clubs or encased in overcoats of concrete, culminating in the famous St. Valentine's Day slaughter in Chicago, when a whole covey of *commerçants* in the liquor trade was rounded up in a garage and machine-gunned to death. Police against criminals found us decently on the side of law and order, but bootleggers and gangsters knocking off other bootleggers and gangsters came under the head of sheer diversion, particularly since the supply seemed to be unlimited.

IX

Also there was a delicious sense of participation. Liquor buyers were held to be lawbreakers as well as liquor sellers. True, we rarely came in contact with the Executive Presidents or Chairmen of the Board of the firms from whom we bought our booze, but there always was a chance that good old Pete or Joe or Sam, who delivered our Scotch or gin, might turn up on page one, propped up for the photographers, his familiar visage pockmarked by bullet holes.

Illegal drinking, at least in the metropolitan centers, became part of the American way of life, and it seemed as though overnight we became a community of souses, living and seeing things either through a bright, poisonous, alcoholic haze or darkly through the worst hangovers imaginable.

We have forgotten how compulsive drinking was, how before dinner or going to the theater one tanked up on questionable martinis and even more questionable Scotch, downing twice the amount one normally would have swallowed because one never knew from where one's next drink would come. The speakeasy where one was known might have been shuttered overnight. And we don't like to recall, either, that hundreds of thousands of us daily committed the indescribable vulgarity of carrying a supply on our persons in hip flasks. Teenagers took to it much in the same way as they are now looking to psychedelic drugs, and I remember one New Year's Eve rout at a place called Gedney Farms in White Plains where young girls of fifteen, sixteen and seventeen were carried screaming from the premises, half blinded by the poisons they had been downing, which included perfume, Bay Rum or anything containing alcohol.

Those who were continually drinking bootleg liquor were far from normal during that period, and only those wealthy and powerful enough to know that they were swallowing genuine imports brought in by offshore operators or midnight lorry transport from Canada could be sure as to what they were putting into their stomachs. Most of us were consistently poisoned.

If one were looking for an insignia to characterize the decade, one might unhesitatingly put up the dollar sign. For during that time there occurred also the biggest, swingiest money boom in our history, when dollars multiplied themselves like bacteria in mold, and I remember that even my office boy in the sports department of the *News* was playing the stock market.

This stock market, which prior to that time had been the private gambling pit of the pirates, robber barons and mystery men of the world of finance, suddenly became a public lottery in which there were no losing numbers, a money pool into which you had only to dip your hands to extract greenbacks, a wonderful dream come true of something for nothing, wealth without work.

There are those who speak of the Twenties as an era of disillusionment, yet what an illusion we entertained in this cockeyed financial area. Looking back upon those times, it is hard to believe that sane people could have cherished it. You bought shares on a margin of ten percent down, waited ten days while the magic market bubbled as you slept, then sold and pocketed a thousand dollars for which you had not lifted a finger. There was only one way for the Dow Jones index to move, and that was up.

The great sports figures of the era added to the golden dream; Gene Tunney earned a million dollars in a night in the ring with Dempsey; Ty Cobb of the Detroit Tigers became the first ballplayer millionaire. Proportionately, golfers, football players, tennis stars, and every other kind of professional athlete were rolling in money. With the advent of the films, for the first time even writers were waxing wealthy, while the celluloid producers were raking in money hand over fist. Books, plays, scripts coined fortunes. Shopgirls turned overnight into moving-picture stars. Singers, dancers, musicians, actors and actresses were making more money than they had ever dreamed existed. Income tax was minimal. Such was the opulence of the new rich who became known as Café Society that their speakeasy hosts could afford to give away nightly bottles of champagne, perfume and other gifts to their patrons and still show out-of-proportion profits.

The magic market was not the only goldmine. The Florida boom was on, and in a welter of circus publicity—swimming pools, fashion parades and bathing girls, band leaders and shimmy dancers— seaside lots rocketed in value beyond belief. In an article in *American Heritage*, George Tindall quotes Kenneth Roberts telling of a strip in Palm Beach which was sold in 1915 for $84,000; in 1922 for $240,000; in 1923 for $800,000; in 1924 for $1,500,000; and in 1925 was estimated to be worth nearly $5,000,000. A New York bank clerk who went to Florida with $1,000 returned three weeks later with $375,000. A New York cab driver drove a passenger who could not get train accommodations all the way to Miami. He stayed there and made a fortune speculating with the money he made driving his cab.

It is neither possible, nor my intention, to attempt a characterization of the Twenties in an introductory article for a book of photographs of personalities, but rather to set the stage for their appearance here and the importance that we attributed to them. One thing is sure: in the decade immediately following upon the Armistice until the crash of the stock market brought it to a close, we were all on one big, damn fine spree.

There was a certain amount of self-pity and certainly a great deal of self-indulgence involved in this. We suffered the delusion that we had won a great war and, excepting for individual casualties, had come out of it unscathed, completely ignoring the years of sacrifice of our allies that made it possible for our last-minute entrance to tip the scales. We felt we had been brave, valorous, adventurous, and gay and reckless in the face of death, and that now the world owed us something singularly characterized in America by the phrase "a good time." Only a handful understood that the war and whatever sacrifices we had made for it had won us nothing—that the world was in a worse muddle than it had been in before, and that the euphoria of the next ten years was the worst hallucination of all.

I was able to share in all this excitement because during that period I was a sportswriter, columnist, sports editor and onetime assistant managing editor of the *News*, the liveliest tabloid on the streets.

The little group of columnists and editors formed a strange elite during that period, a position exalted beyond all intelligent concept and based purely upon the fact that we had free tickets to dispense sometimes, and supposedly inside information on forthcoming contests. The majority of the inmates of this volume I knew or had met personally during my travels in search of sports drama, at

Billy Lahiff's Tavern, "21," the Stork Club, Madison Square Garden ringside, Yankee Stadium, the Polo Grounds, Forest Hills, or any Open Golf Championship, for many of them were lunatic sports fans. Part of the duties of any third-string writer doing "crowd" at a heavyweight championship prize fight was to enumerate the celebrities found ensconced in the first few rows, which always read like a *Who's Who* of stage, screen, literary, gangster and café society.

Next to being able to wave at Jack Dempsey and call out, "Hi-ya, Jack!" it was considered a social asset to know sportswriters. And stars of the caliber of Grantland Rice, W. O. McGeehan, Damon Runyon and Bill Corum were courted as prophets. The fact that my own prognostications as to the outcome of a fight or baseball or football game were utterly worthless didn't prevent the great and the near great from consulting me—"Who do you like, Paul?"

Sportswriters seemed to be immediately accepted in all circles with first-name camaraderie. If they had read us, they knew us—taxi drivers, socialites, bootleggers, gang executioners, merchants' actors and directors. There were very few celebrities in almost any field who did not have some interest in some game.

But over and beyond these personal involvements in whatever it might be—golf, tennis, bowling, horseracing—the spread of interest in the major sports was colossal and unprecedented. Boxing, baseball, football and tennis widened their audiences not so much because of the contests but rather because of the characters who emerged from them, such as Babe Ruth, Dempsey, Tunney, Sharkey, Tilden, Helen Wills, Bobby Jones, Walter Hagen, who not only were dramatic figures as competitors but whose private lives were a continuing serial more thrilling than any to be found in the magazines of the day. People who could not tell a left hook from a lob were still fascinated by these extraordinary practitioners who lived in the public prints. We were their Boswells and often their personal friends. We traveled with them and reported every bit of news about them we could ferret out.

I went to the theater a great deal and to concerts. In preparing this book I was surprised to find how many of the plays mentioned in my research I had seen, how often I had applauded the actors and actresses herein.

My circle happened to be even wider owing to the fact that my father was a well-known musician and pianists, violinists, conductors and composers were entertained in our home. Furthermore, while working my way through Columbia University I spent two seasons as an usher at the Metropolitan Opera House. And yet another group was opened to me when I was sparking a beautiful girl in the Village and so was able to rub shoulders with the newly liberated crowd of artists and writers—and, of course, the parties of Nickolas Muray.

And since before turning to sportswriting I started life as a reviewer of moving pictures in the old "silent" days, during that time I saw them all in action, the girls and boys on their way to stardom.

The decade also earned its characterization as "the time of disillusionment" because a few artists, literati and intellectuals saw through the sham and humbug of the postwar American way of life and crossed the Atlantic to Paris to live there in the *soi disant* superiority of the sham and humbug of the postwar French way of life.

XII

But while these ex-patriots were vocal, they were no more than a few dozen, and the great majority of us were indulging in the gaudiest wingding of our history and one never to be repeated, since the conditions for it could never again be the same. Since we went into World War II disillusioned, the party that followed was in a lower key and never attained the heights of splendid and gilded idiocy of that first postwar binge. Older, wiser and cynical, we tried and are trying to achieve nepenthe through total license and abandonment to the seamy side of life.

In the Twenties, when first the female knee was exposed to us by the flapper, when the one-piece bathing suit revealed a glimpse of thigh and sex became a discussable parlor topic, we were rather more innocent and naively enthusiastic about it all than dirty-minded. We were only half emancipated, still unworldly and un-sex-weary, which meant that, unlike today, there were yet some mysteries and tabus to furnish excitement and titillation. The bedroom window curtains were only half raised and there was still something left to be explored.

Most of the proprieties were being observed. We were not using four-letter words from stage and screen or filling our books with them; humor was not sick; heroes were not anti; hopes were not dashed and romance was still alive. And, above all, there was laughter, as some of the greatest clowns past or present flourished in the theater and on the films, and there was no leer in the laughter. Half-baked we may have been, but it was an exciting and wonderful time in which to have lived.

This was something of our background in the days when the people in this book were famous and their pictures were taken by Nickolas Muray.

MEMENTO MURAY

THE late Nickolas Muray was a Hungarian first and a photographer second.

In Hungarianism—that is to say, the love of life, gregariousness, the artistic eye, diversity of mediums and interests, love of food and entertaining—he was strictly professional. It was only in photography and fencing that he continued to insist that he was an amateur, and of the former his own self-analysis was, "As a photographer, I am just a good plumber."

This was probably because to his work with the camera each time, no matter what the subject, he brought the fresh enthusiasm and excitement of the amateur, and late in life he was still working over each photograph as fondly and meticulously as though it were the first he had ever taken. He was undeniably an artist and equally a first-class photographer. He was also a photo-engraver, pioneer of color photography and color filters, dance critic, Greenwich Village party-giver and a national and international three-weapons champion with foil, *épée* and saber.

Frank Crowninshield, himself one of the outstanding characters of the Twenties, wrote the following about so-called artistic photography and Muray's approach:

"We have been hearing a good deal of nonsense of late about what is called 'artistic photography.' By the same token, there is a good deal of nonsense about 'artistic photography' itself.

"For it is an easy thing to give to a photograph the appearance of a painting, of something 'artistic,' of, let us say, a dancer by Degas, or a nocturne by Whistler. With clever retouching almost anything can be done to a negative or to the reproduction of a photographic print. Name your favorite painter, and any adroit photographer will promise to match that painter's flavor for you, his spirit, and his poetic essence—and all on an ordinary photographic negative.

"The greatest art in photography, of course, comes not from changing nature (a person, a landscape or an inanimate thing) but from showing it truly and simply and from imbuing it with beauty, clarity and dignity. So that, in the last analysis, the most artistic photographs are quite often the simplest and the clearest.

"True art in photography results only from our finding, in a photographer, an inspired devotion to composition, balance, arrangement, lighting and an honest desire to abide by the truth that inheres in his subject.

"The enumeration of these qualities brings us quite naturally to the work of Nickolas Muray, an artist in New York who for many years has managed—notwithstanding an unbelievable volume of work and despite the rapidity with which many of his portraits and assignments have of necessity to be fulfilled—to impart to his work great technical mastery, a disarming honesty and a very considerable degree of beauty. There is nothing of the charlatan in Muray, or in his work; nothing of the poseur, nothing of the man who likes to dim, sugar or distort Life.

"And, because of all these major qualities in him, he has rendered us a high service in furthering the best and most honest traditions of his profession."

This was Nick to the life; no chi-chi, no corduroy pants, smock, flowing tie or flitting about the studio, but simply a dedicated operator in ordinary street clothes getting down to the business of cozening his subject into the illusion that he was in the studio only to discuss his, the sitter's, favorite topic, whether it be music, painting, theater, philosophy or gadgetry, instead of having his picture taken.

Muray's absorption with the sitters was such that he practically resented the photographic apparatus as an interference, and, shedding his coat, rolling up his sleeves and loosening his tie, he treated the actual photographic operation so perfunctorily that his victim was lulled into a false sense of security. Surely no man who appeared to be so raffishly diffident and casual about lights, set-up, focusing and the camera itself could be on the verge of taking a picture.

A man or woman probed for biographical details of youth and past will lie, invent, conceal and embellish. The sitter for a famous photographer, as noted, will endeavor to do the same with his physical self.

Muray had his own way of breaking through, for, unlike many artists whose lives are grimly wrapped up in their work, he was a gay, laughing, cultured fellow and a psychologist as well, who could chatter upon almost any subject.

He had a number of tricks for unlocking rigid jaws and loosening shoulder blades, and one of his most simple secrets was posing people so that they didn't know they were being posed, based upon the kinship between human beings and the banderlog—in other words: *Monkey see, monkey do.* If the client was to occupy a chair, Muray would sit there first while chatting, assuming the attitude he wished from the sitter. A few moments later the latter would be asked to occupy the seat. In nine cases out of ten, he would imitate Nick's posture and half the battle was won with never a word being spoken or even a suggestion having been made.

Muray's work and fame extended into the Sixties and he was still active at the time of his death in 1965. But as a photographer of notables he was a child of the Twenties and an integral part of that era in New York, particularly in the little Bohemia of the city, Greenwich Village. There, for the first time in the history of American culture, a group of creative individuals threw off the shackles of prudery, inhibition and rigidity and established their own Paris Left Bank in the heart of Manhattan.

He was born, however, in Szeged, Hungary, on February 15, 1892, the son of a post-office employee in Budapest. At the age of twelve he was sent to a school for graphic arts, where he learned the fundamentals of photography, photo-engraving and lithographing and at the end of his apprenticeship received an International Engraver's Certificate. Leaving Budapest for Berlin, he perfected himself in advanced color photo-engraving and the manufacture of color filters, an art which was to stand him in good stead in later life.

In 1913 he wrote to a cousin in America, bought a second-class ticket and landed in New York in August of that year with $25 and fifty words of English. Two years later he was doing color separation

and halftone negatives as a union operator with the Condé Nast Company, never dreaming that he would one day be employed by them as a top-rank photographer of world celebrities. Three years of night school made up for Muray's lack of education and, furthermore, equipped him with English spoken without the trace of an accent.

Photography, however, remained his first love, and all through these years his union hours gave him time to study and perfect himself. He was always taking pictures of his friends which somehow seemed to turn out not like any pictures anyone else was making. But when he applied for a job in a photographer's studio, he was told that he was too far out; portraiture at that time was limited to the fixed smile, the pearly teeth and the retouched wrinkles.

A photographer friend, himself a portraitist, advised Muray on the strength of his portfolio to set up shop for himself. Muray did so, and the place where he opened his studio was a house at 129 MacDougal Street, in Greenwich Village, a neighborhood to which everyone was flocking who had a new idea or who was fed up with the old way of doing things.

This was in 1920. The decade characterized by Westbrook Pegler as ''the era of wonderful nonsense'' was about to begin, and in almost no time Nick was selling pictures to the *New York Tribune's* gravure section and *Harper's Bazaar*. His first big sitting was with Florence Reed, then starring in *The Mirage*. You will find the study he made of this actress on page 233. Nick was off and running. The die was cast. He quit photo-engraving, and during the decade that followed hardly anybody worth noting was missing from Muray's coverage of the theatrical, literary, musical and artistic worlds. Besides which, Nick had become *the* Village photographer and *a* Village character whose Wednesday-night studio parties were invariably a cross-section of celebrities from both uptown and downtown.

A contemporary diarist by the name of Angelina, writing in one of the smart magazines, recounts the night that two friends (''Tubby and Edward are such dears . . .'') took her on a slumming tour of the Village, introducing her to The Pepper Pot, Sonia's, The Blue Horse, Barney Gallant's Greenwich Village Inn and, of course, Don Dickerman's The Pirate's Den.

At this point, practically breathless, La Angelina wrote: ''By then it was almost twelve, and since it was a Wednesday, just the hour to drop in at Nickolas Muray's off the Square. Nickolas Muray's Wednesday nights are celebrated—the whole artistic world and his wife can be seen there sometime during the winter. We found the lights out, and everyone gathered round a huge open fire, while Tato Nachio, the South American pianist, played. . . . Ina Claire was in the group, and Willy Pogany, and Serbian Desha, the dancer, and as many more celebrities whom I haven't space to tell—

''And so home—the three of us . . . around one a.m. vowing to the inconstant moon to come back Villagewards as soon as possible.''

It must have been a mild night at Nick's, or the lady left too early or perhaps didn't catch all of the names before running out of space. For there probably were present as well Martha Graham, Ruth St. Denis, Heywood Broun, Sinclair Lewis, Paul Robeson, Carl Van Vechten and Lawrence Langner, not to mention Edna St. Vincent Millay and Eugene O'Neill, Bobby Edwards, Jean

---

XVI

Cocteau, T. S. Eliot, Gertrude Vanderbilt Whitney and Walter Lippmann. Nick knew them all and more. There was food, drink, stimulating conversation and—fencing. For by then Muray was a National Champion, having won the United States saber title in 1927 and 1928, as well as foil and *épée* team championships, and represented the United States on two Olympic teams. One whole wall of the studio in New York where he worked during the last years of his lifetime was covered with medals and trophies.

It was at the New York Athletic Club and the Fencer's Club that Nick and I used to fence *épée* two or three times a week and I learned to know him as an opponent as well as a friend.

It is truly said that after a few minutes on the strip with steel in one's hand, one knows all about the other fellow's character; whether he is honest, tricky, a bluffer, timid, aggressive, intelligent or inclined to be slow-witted. Sword in hand, Nick revealed all of the characteristics that had taken him to the top professionally, culturally and socially. He was no counterfighter, but went after his man with determination and domination. He was a bundle of nervous energy that could explode out of a deceptive calm into an attack too fast often to be parried. He was as graceful as a ballet dancer; one felt that he loved every moment of mock combat, yet at the same time in friendly bouts his style and technique were tinged with humor and delight, and no one laughed louder or more appreciatively than he when hit and he called a score against himself. Fencing when there are no judges present is a gentleman's game, and Nick was one of the first gentlemen of the sport.

For all of his love for this anachronistic game, Muray was essentially a modern man, passing into an age where the way to the stars was through the air. He took up flying and worked at it until he became a first-class pilot, handling the stick with the same delicacy, precision and control he gained over the saber. At one time a lieutenant in the Knickerbocker Squadron of the Civil Air Patrol, he took innumerable publicity photographs for them.

When Nick went abroad to capture on his plates the personalities of such as George Bernard Shaw, H. G. Wells, Ferenc Molnár and John Galsworthy, he kept a written record.

Muray, like few other photographers of note, was literate as well as graphic. He was the critic for *Dance Magazine*, and he kept notes on many of his sittings—stories and comments which in many cases are as interesting as the portraits themselves. Much of his essential simplicity and humility comes through his prose as, without any attempt at concealment, he tells of the trepidation with which he approached great men. Yet at the same time we see these celebrities of both sexes in the studio or facing his camera and learn a little more about what they were like. Here, for instance, verbatim, are his notes on his sitting with George Bernard Shaw:

"'Mr. Shaw had set the sitting for 9.30 a.m. His home in Adelphi Terrace in London was over the small press which printed most of his books. The building was on an islet in a triangular area, approached by a bridge. When I rang the doorbell, Mr. Shaw himself came down and received me with enthusiasm. Seeing that I was overburdened with camera, film holders, etc., he offered to lend a hand with my equipment and carried my wooden tripod as I followed him up to his study. Here I was introduced to Mrs. Shaw, a lovely middle-aged lady with a charming smile, who said:

"'You two boys have a lot in common. I'll leave you to proceed with your mutual interests.'

"Mr. Shaw was one of the founders of the Royal Photographic Society, and was very much interested in photography, in more than an amateur way. He processed his own films and made his own prints. We set up the camera in his study. There were no lights—in those days we used only available light. It was an 8 x 10 view camera with double extension bellows and an old Struss pictorial soft-focus lens. We discussed the pros and cons and pictorial qualities of the camera at length.

"'There were a number of large and medium-sized pianos and piano-type instruments in the study—a spinet and harpsichord among them. I had forgotten that in his youth Shaw had been a music critic, before he started his 'serious' writing. I asked if he knew how to play all these instruments. Thereupon he sat down at the harpsichord and began to play ballads. He sang as well, in not too bad a voice, and seemingly knew endless verses of the old folksongs.

"'He then showed me his albums of photographs he had made with obvious loving care. They were well above amateur standards, and I was happy to praise them quite truthfully. Mrs. Shaw came in—it was then about eleven o'clock—and asked if we would like to have tea. I realized then how fast the time had passed. I was never very good at watching the clock, but reluctantly suggested that we really should take a few pictures before having tea. We had only an hour or so left, since I had a one-thirty appointment with Sir Hall Caine.

"'And so we proceeded with the picture-taking, discussing the lighting and other photographic technicalities as we worked. Shaw was a terrific model. No matter what he did, he was graceful. Almost every picture was interesting, with different expressions, without any self-consciousness. I shot about 18 or 20 negatives before calling it a day. We then sat down to tea and crumpets, which Mrs. Shaw provided. I promised to send him all the proofs in case he wanted any eliminated before I submitted them to *Vanity Fair*, and later did so. He returned them all 'okayed,' but indicated his personal preference among them, asking if I would make a few prints for him. He was kind enough to sign four prints from this sitting for me, which I have in my collection."

The youthful hero worship in Nick reveals itself as well in his encounter with H. G. Wells, of which he writes:

"Long before I met Mr. Wells, I had become one of his devoted admirers. At the 1926 sittings it didn't hurt a bit that I could almost quote him, chapter and verse. I'd been a fan of Jules Verne in my youth, and guess I was just a natural for anyone who attempted to probe the unknown—a truly educated forerunner of what we now call science or space fiction. Almost always I was nervously talkative in the early stages of a sitting with a stranger, unless, of course, the sitter took and held the stage immediately. Mr. Wells greeted me with reserve and dignity, and I fell back on my old habit of trying to get my subject to relax by talking about his work, surroundings, anything which would evoke easy, characteristic expressions. As often happens, one thing led to another, and Mr. Wells began questioning me about cameras and camera techniques. He was much interested in color photography, then in an experimental stage. It happened that I'd been fooling around with color in Germany and in England, and so was able to tell him quite a bit about it.

XVIII

"At one point in the sitting a loose screw on my camera bothered me, and I pulled from my pocket a rather curious knife which had been given me by a gadgeteer friend. Among other oddments the knife held a small screwdriver. Wells asked to examine the knife; the conversation was entirely about crazy tools and Rube Goldberg-type inventions. I knew Goldberg and tried to give Wells a verbal picture of that wonderful man.

"The sitting lasted far beyond the time allotted. We finally parted with a warm handshake and mutual promises to meet again soon."

But Nick in Celebrity Land was not only meeting famous men; he was also coming up against the great feminine beauties and characters, and a slight note of little-boy dismay and embarrassment combined with "Whoopee! Get me!" excitement is evident. Amongst his papers after his death were his impressions of such as Carole Lombard, Marlene Dietrich and Greta Garbo.

On a trip to Hollywood, Nick had been assigned to photograph Miss Lombard for the cover of a magazine, and the appointment was set for an empty film studio stage.

"The layout called for a royal blue hostess gown, but Miss Lombard came out of her dressing room in a bright red one. As she came across the stage, she exchanged greetings with the grips, electricians and other workers in the most vivid and earthy language I'd ever heard from the lips of a woman. For some reason it didn't seem in the least bit vulgar, perhaps because a mutual affection was so obvious. Upon introduction we were instantly on first-name terms, and I felt as if I'd known her for a long, long time. I mentioned the layout's color requirement, whereupon Carole launched into a tirade at the bumbling of publicity "brass." She undid the gown and threw it to the floor, standing before us without a stitch on except her high-heeled shoes. She enjoyed getting a rise out of people, and would go to any length including shock tactics to achieve a laugh."

Muray caught the great Dietrich, whom Hemingway always fondly referred to as "the Kraut," in one of her *Hausfrau* moods:

"Miss Dietrich asked that I photograph her at her home. I arrived half an hour early so that I might set up ahead of time and be ready for her. The door was opened by a rather unkempt woman with no make-up, dressed in slacks and a shirt with rolled-up sleeves. It wasn't until she greeted me by name that I realized it was Miss Dietrich herself. I must have turned all colors—certainly I was greatly embarrassed. She, however, didn't turn one untidy hair. She suggested I look around to see where I'd like the photograph taken while she dressed.

"To my delight, I found a magnificent Gauguin original hanging in the living room. By the time I'd placed my lights and camera, a vision was coming down the stairs. Miss Dietrich was beautiful, and beautifully natural. The Gauguin in the background provided the final touch for this portrait, which I consider one of my best."

Nick's word picture of Garbo was equally revealing:

"Greta Garbo is one of the most beautiful women it has ever been my privilege to photograph.

"At MGM they assigned me to an open studio which was not being used, and set up the very simple background I selected. Next to this stage a set was being constructed for some movie. The date

XIX

was for one o'clock. I had asked that she wear a décolleté evening gown, because what I had in mind for the full page was a close-up, with just head and shoulders. As usual, I arrived ahead of time to set up my camera and lights. Howard Strickling, head of publicity for MGM, arrived a few minutes early and began to talk about Garbo. He told me that their experience with her for publicity shots was difficult—not that she was temperamental, but she was unpredictable. Sometimes she would sit for one or two exposures and walk off the set without saying a word. Perhaps she might not show up at all. Usually she was gracious and cooperative with the photographer. It all depended on her mood and the situation.

"We waited for half an hour—forty-five minutes—I began to wonder if the churning in my innards was that overdue ulcer. An hour had passed before she arrived, dressed in a man's shirt, tie and jacket, and a beret. Very apologetically she explained that she had spent all the intervening time in the wardrobe department, trying to find a décolleté evening dress, but couldn't find one to fit. The 'adaptable photographer' assured her that what she had on was just fine. We got to work and I took about a dozen shots, with and without the beret, with and without the jacket, with and without the tie. Then I asked her if she would slip the shirt down a bit so that we could get a close-up of just head and shoulders. With complete cooperation she took off the shirt altogether.

"The noisy set next to our stage became utterly silent. Not even breathing could be heard. Strickling was the first to react.

" 'No, no, Nick! Don't— You can't take a picture like that!' He picked up the shirt and covered her, ordering us to wait until he returned with material to drape over her. While he was gone, we took a few more shots and chatted. She laughed at Howard's concern and said she felt quite at ease posing for me. Then she began asking me about my equipment. She was very interested in the simple lighting set-up I traveled with, and also in the old Struss pictorial lens, which I showed and explained to her. When Howard returned with the drapery, we finished the sitting.

"It is difficult to describe her—that incredible oval-shaped face; blond, strong hair; eyes that engaged you when serious and that made you feel happy when she smiled; the animation as we discussed her various roles, some comic, some tragic, serious and flippant. Her slight accent enhanced her English, which was quite good, and seemed to add both to her seriousness and her kindliness and friendliness."

The first time ever that Douglas Fairbanks and Mary Pickford appeared together in a picture was one only recently celebrated by the teaming of Richard Burton and Elizabeth Taylor, *The Taming of the Shrew*. Through an old friend, Frank Case, owner of the famous Algonquin Hotel in New York, Muray was invited to photograph them on the set. Here are his jottings on skylarking in the studios:

"We arrived early, so that I could get the 'feel' of the shots I wanted. Each day the stars invited friends to watch the shooting, or the publicity people brought in a few VIP's. In any case, there was always a small audience, who were seated in a single row containing about twenty-five chairs. The chairs seemed to be made of old-fashioned mahogany, but were in reality made of metal. When the take was finished, Doug and Mary bowed and went off to their dressing rooms. While we waited for

XX

them to return, Doug was busy changing his costume and putting on a mustache. He strolled onto the set looking like one of the gaffers or electricians, and busied himself with examining one of the lights. Then he strolled off, about 15 or 20 feet behind the guest chairs. He carried a long rod which was connected with an electrical outlet. As he casually passed behind us, he touched our chairs with the tip of the rod, producing a rude shock to the sitters. There was much shrieking and then laughter when we found out what had happened. The only person who didn't jump was Frank Case, who was sitting next to me at the end of the row. I turned to him, almost in anger, and asked him why. 'Well, Nick,' he said, 'I've been here many times. I know this routine. Before I come here I always put on rubber pants.'

"Frank introduced me to Doug as the photographer who'd come out to shoot him for *Vanity Fair*. Doug said, 'I know—but he's a fencer too.' That year I'd won the National saber championship, but it never occurred to me that he'd know about this. Of course I offered to practice with him any time he'd like to do so. He said, 'Oh no, no, no—I'm not in your class. I'm strictly a stage fencer.'

"He was one of the very few actors I've ever known to admit this. Stage fencing goes to rhythm, much as a singer sings a song. The action is nowhere near as violent as it appears on the screen, but is done to a rhythm—one, two, three, four; one, two, three, four. Instead of 24 frames a second, they work to one-eighth of a second, which on the screen is speeded up three times as fast as they actually perform the motions. If they actually fenced at the speed of a regular take, great danger would be involved, particularly with actors who are inexperienced or inept at fencing. So, what looks murderous on the screen is in reality a very tame performance.

"Doug was also being modest. We became good friends and fenced together many times. A natural athlete, he was a much better fencer than lots of opponents I've faced in competitions. Young Doug, his son, was also a pretty good fencer. I thoroughly enjoyed fooling around with both of them in sword play."

Muray was a genuine ballet buff, an old firehorse of the dance, and there was rarely a studio party that did not feature as well as fencing a performance by one or another or pairs of his dancing friends. Of these his favorites were Ruth St. Denis and her husband, Ted Shawn. Among Nick's papers we found the following:

"Miss Ruth and I have had a love affair going for over forty years. She's still doing well-publicized yoga headstands in her eighties, and not too long ago I saw a recital advertised for her with one of my photographs from the Twenties. I doubt that results today would differ much from these pictures of long ago.

"The Denishawn school of dancing was one of the biggest sources of joy for me. Their interpretive program featured great variety—different periods and different nationalities all around the world, from the Greeks to the Persians to the Japanese to the Middle East to the South Pacific to the Spaniards, and then to traditional American dancing to include the American Indians. Ted's repertoire included African, Egyptian, Turkish and Byzantine. Miss Ruth could and did do anything.

"Ted was an outstanding teacher. He was uniquely able to express beauty with both body and mind, and could transplant his ideas and ideals into his students. Jacob's Pillow, their studio in Massachusetts, has become a Denishawn monument, with an international festival each summer. Ted's students vie with famous dancers from Mexico, Europe, Russia and elsewhere. The greatest American dancers and choreographers—Charles Weidman, Doris Humphrey, Agnes de Mille, Martha Graham—on and on, ad infinitum—were graduates or disciples of Miss Ruth and Ted. I photographed them all, together with anyone else who made a pretense of dancing.

"Some months ago I met Miss Ruth at the Metropolitan Opera House. Some ballet or other was going on. She threw her arms around me and gave me a resounding smack, to the edification of the on-lookers. Then she said, and this I treasure, that both she and Ted were still using my old photos for current publicity!"

Muray's encounter with one of his bosses, Bernarr Macfadden, was unmitigated comedy, for the late Bernarr was a physical-culture nut, an exhibitionist quite in keeping with the dreadful tabloid he fathered amongst other dreadful publications, but there was no doubt that he was a vital and intriguing figure of the era.

Macfadden's connection with Muray was that he was the publisher of *Dance* Magazine, for which, as noted, Muray wrote as well as photographed. But let Nick tell it:

"For two years I was critic and reviewer for *Dance* Magazine, attending all recitals and commenting thereon for the magazine. I had long been interested in the dance and in dancers, and had an enviable collection of photographs of the stars of that day. This new assignment brought me even more sitters.

"Macfadden's secretary called to make an appointment for a portrait of HIMSELF for his *Physical Culture* Magazine. He was at the time about sixty-one or sixty-two years old, well preserved, with bushy white hair. He was a little man, about 5′7″, and, as so often happens, had the psyche of a giant.

"Macfadden arrived at about ten o'clock for his sitting, and asked if I had received his clipping books. I had not. Immediately he took possession of the phone and with much violent language ordered them sent over by messenger. Shortly thereafter a very young and skinny girl arrived with two clipping books, one under each arm. She was fairly staggering beneath the weight. I took the books into the studio and sat down on the bench to look over them with him. They were all pictures from his early youth up to date, made on behalf of physical culture—thighs, shoulders, arms, legs— endless muscles, everything enhanced (or the reverse) by Greek costumes, with gladiator shoes and tigerskin uppers.

"I have rarely spent a more boring half-hour than I did while skimming through these books. When I asked why on earth he had bothered sending them, he replied that he'd liked my pictures for his various publications, mostly *Dance* Magazine. He wanted me to make action pictures of him— 'strip-pitchas'—and I must not make anything like the stereotyped photographs in his clipping books. I asked him if he meant nude studies, and he said he did. Well, there was my dressing room—I told him to take his things off and we would proceed.

"Five minutes later Macfadden came out—clad in the tigerskin and gladiator shoes he'd smuggled in via his briefcase, just exactly as he looked in the clippings he scorned. I became, for once, a temperamental artist. I shouted at him that he must take everything off if I was to make figure studies. He returned to the dressing room. Back he came, with a jockstrap and the gladiator shoes. I shook my head and told him I could not do him justice unless I had his full cooperation. I had taken out from my bookcase a volume of Michelangelo's drawings for the Sistine Chapel, and I showed these to Macfadden. There were no costumes, of course, and this was exactly what he wanted. He went back to the dressing room. This time he emerged without jockstrap or shoes, but holding his hand to cover his masculine part. I said, 'You don't have to be shy with me, Mr. Macfadden—just be yourself, as if you were all alone. I'm nonexistent, a piece of apparatus to record your magnificent body.'

"Before I finished saying this, he was on the floor doing push-ups, and I yelled at him to stop. Michelangelo's poses were difficult and strenuous, but these were what he wanted. The first was a three-quarter profile, with knees up and shoulders placed parallel with the camera—a terrific twist for him to hold. He was a glutton for punishment, and held every pose until the sweat poured.

"We took about sixteen or eighteen negatives. I processed them myself and sent the proofs to Macfadden. I had a personal telephone call from him after he looked them over. He said, 'Well, these are certainly the kind of pictures I hoped to get someday—and here it is, the day has arrived.'

"Then he asked if I would do him a favor. Would I write an article about the sitting? The idea, of course, was to flatter this young sixty-two-year-old man and praise his efforts throughout his life to preserve a young body for his age. I agreed to do the best I could, and my secretary corrected the English of my manuscript.

"The February issue of *Physical Culture* featured my pictures. To my surprise, all the nudes were retouched and thereby covered with the tried and true leopardskin costume."

Many of the famous of those days met for the first time at one of Muray's studio parties or during sittings, and his memoirs on his association with Eugene O'Neill record one that ended in a tragedy: the suicide of Ralph Barton, the illustrator and caricaturist. This was a particularly painful event, since Barton was one of Muray's best friends, and, as he recounts, it all started in his studio. But first he presents an unusual portrait of America's greatest playwright:

"I first met Eugene O'Neill around 1919, when I had my studio next to the Provincetown Players on MacDougal Street and photographed some of the productions he had written or directed.

"O'Neill had invited me to his home on the Cape, an old lighthouse on the outskirts of Provincetown. There were two ways to reach it—by boat through the ocean, or by foot through two miles of loose sand. Henriette Metcalf, Drama Editor of *Vanity Fair*, and I chose the latter route, and turned up weary beyond belief, laden as we were with tripod, 8 x 10 view camera, and accessories. However, we were both young and quickly recovered from the difficult trip. We were received with great affection and an elaborate luncheon. The afternoon's sitting was as much play as it was work. I used my 8 x 10 camera and also a lowly Brownie for action pictures. The shot he liked best, and which was to be the picture he used most, was taken with the Brownie, at the lighthouse on top of the dunes.

XXIII

"At that time O'Neill was married to Agnes Boulton. They had one child then, the boy Shane. My camera recorded them all. Gene was a champion swimmer with a splendid body and beautiful athletic form. He was as playful as a dolphin in the water, which made for exciting pictures as he disappeared beneath the sea and reappeared spouting water. He might, under other circumstances, have been an Olympic kayak star. The rough seas on the Cape challenged him to do his best in this fragile craft.

"When the pictures had been taken, we took time out for a picnic on the sand. Baskets appeared from nowhere, with drinks, sandwiches and sweets. Gene was to prove a fine host through the years.

"My next picnic with O'Neill was in Bermuda, where he had built or, rather, rebuilt a beautiful house. I made the trip with John Held and Billy Prince and their respective wives, and we were all invited to a cook-out at O'Neill's shore home. By then Oona was on the scene, a pretty little thing, adored by all. The water was somewhat chilly, but that didn't stop Gene from dashing in and displaying his athletic prowess. I took many stills and also motion pictures of this fantastically interesting man with his family and friends. He was completely photogenic, with the figure of a young and vigorous athlete. He and John Held and Billy Prince became friends immediately, as I knew they would. There was much rough-housing and later much in the way of serious talk."

At Muray's next meeting with Eugene O'Neill, Fate played as romantically cruel and inexorable a part as it often did in the playwright's own dramas. The time was mid-decade:

"In 1925 I had an appointment with him for new pictures which his publishers, Boni & Liveright, wanted. The appointment was made for eleven o'clock. That same morning I had another sitter, Carlotta Monterey, who was then the wife of Ralph Barton, the illustrator, writer and cartoonist, and an old friend. She was about to open as the star of O'Neill's *Hairy Ape*. Carlotta was late and her sitting ran past eleven o'clock. Gene was prompt, even a little early for his sitting. I asked Carlotta if she would mind having him as an audience instead of keeping him waiting in the reception room. She said of course I should bring him in. He liked the idea, and watched me direct Mrs. Barton in the various poses she planned to use for publicity purposes.

"When I finished with Carlotta, she asked O'Neill if he would mind her watching me photograph him. Of course he had no alternative except to reply that although this was breaking all precedents, she was welcome to watch if she didn't find it boring. She didn't.

"Gene's sitting took something less than an hour. We knew what we wanted and got it quickly. At that point I was hungry and asked both of them if they would join me for lunch at the Crillon. I knew the owner there, and we were given a corner table. The conversation was about the theater and costumes, as I remember. This casual acquaintance grew as I watched. Both Gene and Carlotta were engrossed. I had an afternoon sitting, and apologized for leaving them to go back to the saltmines. They couldn't have cared less. I didn't know then that this was the beginning of a romance which culminated in Carlotta divorcing Ralph Barton and Gene divorcing Agnes. They were married shortly thereafter.

"The compound tragic ending came in 1930, when Ralph returned from Paris. I photographed him the day before he committed suicide. His self-written obituary mentioned that Carlotta refused to come back to him, giving that as the reason for his desperate decision."

Nick always laughed at himself as a writer and he would have been half embarrassed and half amused at my quoting verbatim from his notes. He always thought it funny that people actually paid him for his compositions, even though he took a sly pride in the fact that he received sometimes as much as two and a half cents a word.

It was all a part of Hungarianism. His most trenchant revelations of some of the greats and near greats of the Twenties were, of course, obtained through his technical mastery of the apparatus of photography and his personal approach to and understanding of his sitters. This, then, is his book and herewith his results.

XXV

THE PORTRAITS

THE PORTRAITS

THE REVEALING EYE

GEORGE ABBOTT

GEORGE ABBOTT, who at the age of eighty today has not changed a great deal from this young, steely-eyed actor, playwright, director, producer of the Twenties, was the improbable prototype of the country boy from Salamanca, New York, who became Mr. Broadway.

Forty-one years ago this man, who as a youth had been a ranch hand in Cheyenne and a Western Union messenger rushing growlers for the *mesdames* of the red-light district, revolutionized the American theater with his co-authoring and directing of the ultra-sophisticated melodrama *Broadway*.

At the time Mr. Abbott came to The Street, the American theater was emerging from its turn-of-the-century phase of costume dramas and essential innocence, when such plays as *The Old Homestead*, *Zaza*, *If I Were King*, *Beau Brummell*, *Dolly Varden* and *The College Widow* had vied for attention with Primrose and Dockstader's Minstrels and such musical extravaganzas as *The Wizard of Oz*, *Babes in Toyland* and *The Sultan of Sulu*.

The stars of those earlier days were Sarah Bernhardt, Mrs. Leslie Carter, William Gillette, Margaret Anglin, Minnie Maddern Fiske, Maude Adams, Weber and Fields, Richard Mansfield, the Four Cohans and Mrs. Patrick Campbell, with, of course, a particular bow to Lillian Russell.

Twenty years later, with Mr. Abbott on the scene serving his apprenticeship as a young actor, the names (with the exception of Mme. Bernhardt) were different and Eugene O'Neill had made his first impact upon modern drama with *Beyond the Horizon* and *The Emperor Jones*. Jeanne Eagels was appearing in *Rain*, and Pauline Lord in *Anna Christie*. The Astaires were dancing, John Barrymore was the great tragedian, and for fun and girls the *Ziegfeld Follies* were with us—*and* Mr. Abbott.

He came at a period when, with the theater in a state of flux and producers uncertain of themselves, it seemed almost a miracle that so much talent could be embodied in one man. Between the years 1920 and 1930 he acted in, directed, wrote, co-authored, produced or play-doctored twenty-two plays, of which *The Fall Guy*, *Love 'Em and Leave 'Em*, *Broadway*, *Chicago*, *Coquette*, *Gentlemen of the Press* and *Jarnegan* each took his contemporary theater further along the road to modernization.

FRANKLIN P. ADAMS

IN Chicago the initials were B.L.T.; in New York, F.P.A. They stood for two of the most famous literary men of the day—Bert Leston Taylor of the *Chicago Tribune*, and Franklin Pierce Adams of the *New York World*. And of the two, Adams as diarist and erudite arbiter amongst the town's would-be literati was the more interesting and exciting personality. He was to go on in his later years to become a radio and television character on *Information Please*, recognized by millions. But in the Twenties he was known only as the editor, conductor and paragrapher of a column entitled *The Conning Tower*.

The Conning Tower, unlike most of the columns of today, was a delight to the eye as well as to the intellect. Couplets, quatrains, jingles, short light verse alternated with pithy and witty paragraphs. It was never dull, always stimulating or entertaining.

And it was wholly American, sprung from general-store, cracker-barrel humor, the short, sharp, salty quip that Will Rogers developed on the stage while men like Frank Adams and Bert Taylor became the ringmasters of daily literary circuses in the newspapers.

We were then, too, first becoming aware of some of the more blatant hypocrisies by which we had been living, and the country was producing men like H. L. Mencken, Ring Lardner, Sinclair Lewis and F.P.A. to puncture them.

Frank Adams was a wry, earnest, gently cynical man who hated phonies and falseness of any kind and had no patience with ineptness either. He tilted daily at our foibles. He kidded our shibboleths, derided our dogmas and was a past master at cozening the sharpest minds in town to work for him for nothing. He was bombarded daily with hundreds of letters containing contributions of verse, puns, jokes, satiric paragraphs and epigrams, many of them submitted under pseudonyms. He winnowed them ruthlessly and with the most exquisite good taste. To be able to say that you had "made" F.P.A's column and prove it was one of the highest literary accolades of the times.

ZOE AKINS

A Pulitzer Prize winner, Zoe Akins once remarked in an interview, "Women are not fitted for careers. I, who have one, say it.

"Women cannot take things lightly enough," she explained. "Men can drink a little, love a little, laugh a little and keep on working. If women drink at all, they are drunkards. If they love, they do it with an intensity that blots out everything else. They cannot relax.

"There's only one career where perhaps a woman may be happy and successful. Acting is a form of play, and so, without any effort on the part of the actress, work and play are mingled. So the stage perhaps is the one exception to the tragedy of feminine careers."

This from Miss Akins in 1922, poetess, short-story writer, novelist and dramatist—and non-actress.

Oddly enough, Brooks Atkinson once, reviewing one of her plays, wrote, "Probably Zoe Akins should have been on the stage. She is all emotion."

Yet, from the time of her great dramatic success *Déclassée*, in which Ethel Barrymore played in 1919 and which brought Miss Akins her first important recognition, she never exchanged her pen for greasepaint and in that marvelous decade of ours grew in stature year by year. She wrote sixteen plays in sixteen years, including *Daddy's Gone A-Hunting*, *The Texas Nightingale*, *The Moon-Flower*, *First Love*, *The Crown Prince*, *The Love Duel* and *The Greeks Had a Word for It*, building up to her winning of the Pulitzer Prize in 1935 with her dramatization of Edith Wharton's *The Old Maid*.

Her plays were not universal hits; some were more popular than others, but she was always with us. We were aware of the name and fame of Zoe Akins. There was always a play by her either in preparation or running on Broadway. Until her death in October of 1958, she pursued with her sensitive pen that career of all work and very little play which she so decried for women.

CAPTAIN ROALD AMUNDSEN

YOU would want him with you in a tight corner, this sturdy, calm, rugged man with the heavy-lidded eyes, who would know what to do when disaster struck through mountainous waves, blinding blizzard or sub-freezing cold. He was Adventure. He was the immovable rock against which the forces of nature expended themselves, and he was Romance, the last of a breed of explorers whose day was drawing to a close until the coming of the spacemen. For after the time of Captain Roald Amundsen there were few places on the face of the earth upon which man had not set foot.

He lived to broaden men's knowledge of this planet. He died dramatically in service of "Greater love hath no man than this, that a man lay down his life for his friends."

This astonishing Norwegian sea captain bridged two worlds and two eras. He was the first person actually to reach the South Pole, to close out the chapter of polar exploration with ships and dogs that had thrilled earlier generations. Fourteen years later, in 1926, the air age was upon us. Captain Amundsen left behind the stout oak planks of his ships and, with Commander Lincoln Ellsworth of the United States and General Umberto Nobile of Italy, he flew in the Italian dirigible *Norge* over the North Pole from Spitsbergen to Teller on the Bering Sea, after having survived three prior disastesr in attempting journeys by heavier-than-air machines. Two days before this flight Commander R. E. Byrd of the United States Navy flew from Spitsbergen to the Pole and back in sixteen hours. These were the days of the pioneers of long-distance aviation, for the next year Lindbergh was to span the Atlantic.

In 1928 this university-educated seaman did die for his friend. When General Nobile's airship *Italia* was wrecked on a polar flight, Amundsen financed the expedition to search for him. On June 7 he flew off in an airplane northward and the curtains of polar mist and fog closed behind him. Although General Nobile was eventually rescued, Captain Roald Amundsen and his companions vanished and were never heard from again.

JOHN MURRAY ANDERSON AND BARNEY GALLANT

THESE two foreigners symbolize New York's reply to Montmartre and the Left Bank of Paris: Greenwich Village, that little Bohemia situated in the triangle of crooked streets in the heart of Old New York.

John Murray Anderson (seated), stage producer, born in St. John's, Newfoundland, was the director of the first *Greenwich Village Follies*, while the Latvian immigrant Barney Gallant ran the Greenwich Village Inn and a succession of speakeasies and nightclubs. As such, he was the *first* person in the United States to be placed in durance vile for selling a drink in contravention of the Volstead Act.

A gay, happy-go-lucky little man, Barney and his *bistros* called attention to the fact that New Yorkers no longer need ride a ten-day boat to Paris, France, to find themselves in a *milieu* of flowing ties, literary talk, candle-lit cellars, screwball poets and weirdies of every kind. The Village likewise boasted the most sizzling collection of chicks, who had migrated there to knock off the shackles of the double standard and indulge in what was euphemistically and thrillingly known as free love.

Shacking up on Fourth Street was secondary to the street's importance as the caldron of liberalism, socialism and other isms. Nevertheless, adolescent New Yorkers crossed its boundary line to sit tingling with sexual excitement in dimly lit tearooms and tiny cafés, hungrily eyeing the short-haired girls in smocks and sandals who might be free-lovers, but more often turned out to be *Hausfraus* out for an evening's relaxation with their husbands.

The real characters to emerge from this American Bohemia—Eugene O'Neill, Walter Lippmann, Mabel Dodge, Harry Kemp, Maxwell Bodenheim, Carl Van Vechten and others—were not to be found in the artsy-craftsy *boîtes*, but instead at the Liberal Club, Polly's Restaurant and—of course—Barney Gallant's.

DAME JUDITH ANDERSON

GREAT tragediennes from little actresses grow. The most commanding, dignified and powerful voice on the American stage today was only a faint whisper back in the Twenties, yet she was there, this five-foot-four-inch Australian, playing a modest part in the exciting days when our theater began to grow up.

A tiny, gay creature who was ignored by the geniuses of Hollywood during World War I, she came to Broadway. There, from a run-of-the-mill actress appearing in such quickly forgotten opuses as *Peter Weston* with Frank Keenan, *Cobra* and *The Dove* (an affair of shenanigans and banditry in Mexico produced by David Belasco), she made herself over into a tragedienne by trying to drown out the ocean.

Muray recalls the young Judith in two extraordinary situations: One, standing at the edge of the sea on Long Island, rehearsing her dramatic scenes by shouting at the top of her lungs against the thunder of the Atlantic surf and pausing only to inquire of the photographer, "Can you hear me, Nick?" Muray later wrote in his notes, "Thus were the pectoral muscles of the diaphragm hardened and her vocal cords stretched to the farthest balcony. Her voice became penetrating even when she whispered."

The other memory was of the feather-light girl attached by a chain to an enormous harlequin Great Dane, which she walked in Central Park at midnight after the theater, only to find herself flying through the air as the monster, who outweighed her by several pounds, took off after something.

She was a part of the Twenties indeed, but it was a kind of waiting in the wings, partaking of the excitement of the era and preparing for the call to greatness. It was not until the end of the decade, when her developing art became welded to that of another rising genius of the theater, Eugene O'Neill, and she played in *Strange Interlude* and *Mourning Becomes Electra*, that audiences became aware that they had been witnessing the birth of an actress whose depth and power were to dominate the American stage for the next thirty years.

LA ARGENTINA

THE whimsical fancy of Nickolas Muray turned often to catching his celebrities in unconventional poses far removed from their professions, and no one would suspect the smiling lady in the unbecoming flowerpot headgear of her period, sitting on a burro, of being the most passionately exciting and famous Spanish dancer of her time.

Her name was Antonia Mercé, but her stage name was La Argentina, from the country in which she was born during the time that her parents, stars of the Royal Spanish Opera Ballet, were filling an engagement there.

Foot-stamping, castanet-clicking, so-called Spanish dancers had appeared in the United States before, but not until La Argentina did audiences become aware of the fire, diversity and beauty inherent in the art.

Emotion was worrying to the turn-of-the-century Americanos, except where it was bathos ladled out by persecuted matinee heroines or early film stars. Yet it was pure emotion with which La Argentina captivated us. For over and beyond the technical perfection of the folk dances of her land were the personal magnetism and temperament that shone through all her performances. The flash of her eyes, the universal expression of hate, joy, love, fear, anger, impishness, through rhythmic movements of the body and the changes of a mobile face, left those who had come to see merely a "Spanish Dancer" aroused and disturbed.

Nor had anything as stirring as her castanet play been encountered before. She could make them whisper so delicately as to verge upon the soundless, or beat upon the eardrums and vibrate through the system like the clangor of a giant metronome. As she danced, her fingers sang.

As an indication of how rapidly audiences were maturing in the United States in that era: Her first appearances in New York, around 1917, were largely ignored. Ten years later she was accepted as a sensation and her recitals in New York, Chicago and San Francisco sold out.

PETER ARNO

FOR close to half a century Americans have been laughing ruefully at the cartoons of Curtis Arnoux Peters, who signs himself Peter Arno.

The fellow quizzically facing the lens of Nickolas Muray in the mid-Twenties might be captioned "The American Hogarth of the Rich." It was during those mid-Twenties that we, with our newfound society of the cafés, came under that derisive eye, when his cartoons deriding American manners and customs first began to appear in *The New Yorker*. And how this society for so long managed to survive the bite of his wit and the ridicule of his pen is an indication of the extreme durability of idiocy.

Peter Arno followed the golden-spoon trail to stardom on *The New Yorker*. He was the son of a Supreme Court Justice, Hotchkiss graduate and Yale student. Organizer of a dance band known as the Yale Collegians, whose major claim to fame was that it gave to the world Rudy Vallee, he turned from music to his talent for drawing.

The "400" with their social *éclat* and pretensions had sunk from the weight of their own dull ponderousness to be replaced, after the War and during the arid years of Prohibition, by a new class. Its distinction was either the wealth or the celebrity which enabled its members to sit and drink in such famous speakeasies as the Stork Club, "21" and El Morocco. When the Volstead Law was finally expunged from the books, these oases and their veterans survived.

Peter Arno himself was one of these, ruthlessly using as the model for the most devastating cartoons to appear since the days of Thomas Nast the stuffed shirts of his times, whether clad in black or white tie, military uniform or union overalls, debutantes, young men-about-town, judges, lawyers, big shots and dowagers. The only explanation of their endurance under the shattering attack of his full-page drawings and the quips beneath was that the lampooned were his most faithful clients who laughed the loudest. It still goes on today.

FRED AND ADELE ASTAIRE

I N 1932 a brother-and-sister dance team that had been enchanting audiences for some twenty-five years (starting on the Orpheum and Keith circuits when the boy was only seven) broke up when the girl went to London to marry an English lord. Cast loose, the brother set off for Hollywood and was screen-tested. The report, after noting his measurements, was: "Slightly bald; personality negative; dances some; ballroom style." This was Fred Astaire from Omaha, Nebraska, and his sister, who married Lord Charles Cavendish, was Adele, his dancing partner throughout the Twenties in such shows as *For Goodness' Sake*, *The Bunch and Judy*, *Lady, Be Good*, *Funny Face* and *Smiles*.

There is a youngish-looking fellow by that name still dancing on the television screens of the nation who is obviously an impostor, since no one could possibly retain youth, style, class, agility and exquisite perfection over so many years. Yet they do say that this is the same Fred Astaire who, in that long-ago era of the theater between 1920 and 1930, took tap and soft-shoe out of the realm of burlesque and vaudeville and, dressed in white tie, top hat and tails, gave it an elegance, delicacy and polish that appealed to emerging American society.

So impeccable were the dancing Astaires, most of us thought they were British. Adele was pretty, but it was Fred who had the air. He was not at all handsome, with a face too thin and a pointed jaw, but once he was poured into evening clothes with a top hat rakishly slanted on his head, his feet tapped out such perfection as had not yet been seen upon the musical-comedy stage. Talented Adele echoed every movement and with her own peculiar grace. The combination stirred up the strangest feelings of delight and satisfaction in the hearts of their audiences.

TALLULAH BANKHEAD

THE William Brockman Bankheads, of whom Bankhead *père* was Speaker of the House of Representatives, had a daughter Tallulah, who, when she was ten years old, registered displeasure by lying on the floor, kicking and drumming her heels. Sometimes she would hold her breath till her face grew purple and the household panicked, with the exception of Grandma Tallulah, who would sit it out grimly and say, "We've had about enough of that. Throw water on the brat." Tallulah grew up into a character.

She became a capable but not a particularly imposing actress, possessed of a deep voice and slapdash style, but her raucous, extrovert personality was an example of the more strident emancipation of the women of the Twenties who cut their hair short, smoked cigarettes, used language and did as they damn pleased.

Even if the Congressman's daughter had never chosen to elevate the theater, Tallulah would have been some kind of personality or hell-raiser around town, for she was as uninhibited as a South Sea maiden but considerably more noisy. Nevertheless, Tallulah maintained that she was a lady, and what is more, she was.

With her Alabama-born drawl, her booming salutation of "Dahling!", her ebullient generosity and outspokenness, Miss Bankhead didn't need her name in lights on Broadway to be noticed.

She and Muray became close friends, and one of his favorite anecdotes about her was of the day when George S. Kaufman, doctoring a play she was in, called at her apartment by appointment. The door opened to reveal Miss Bankhead barefooted all the way up, with not a stitch on. Mr. Kaufman dead-panned, "Tallulah, your zipper's open."

The lady, however, was far from being a freak in the theater and has won some half a dozen critics' awards for past performances in both films and drama. And if you go to a ballgame around New York today, that foghorn voice you hear rooting might well still be "Tallu."

ETHEL BARRYMORE

WHEN I was a boy growing up around New York during the early 1900's, it was considered smart to say in a sepulchral voice, "That's all there is. There isn't any more." And the majority of the punks who said this didn't even know why, except that it had become a part of the national language like "23 Skidoo" or "Get out and push!" The line was first spoken at the opening night in 1904 of a hit play called *Sunday*, when, to quiet the tumultuous applause at its end, the leading actress, Ethel Barrymore, returned to the stage to make that announcement.

Muray's study of this great queen of the "Royal Family" and descendant of the Drews and the Barrymores, was made in 1926, under curious circumstances. The photographer was a great friend of the bedridden playwright Edward Sheldon, who, though unable to move his arms or legs, was constantly consulted by producers, playwrights and actors, including the Barrymore family. One night Sheldon invited Muray to come to dinner and bring his camera, for after the meal they were going to rehearse Miss Barrymore, who was to appear in Somerset Maugham's *The Constant Wife*. The intense and revealing portrait of the concentration of a great actress is one that resulted from that evening's theatrical workshop.

Her outstanding characteristics from early teens to the end of her life were a tremendous dignity, a deep vibrant voice which plucked unendingly at the heartstrings of the audience, and a regal bearing. She was among the first of the stage stars to become a cult. Because of her intense and tragically moving personality, young girls who haunted the galleries at her matinees tried to copy her voice, her walk and other of her mannerisms.

As with all great actresses, who are ageless, one hardly noticed her transition from roles of glamour to the later mature characterizations such as the schoolmistress of *The Corn Is Green*. Although she retired officially in 1936, she was back on Broadway a year later and never really relinquished the theater until her death at the age of seventy-nine in 1959.

RICHARD BARTHELMESS

IF you were a kid in the Twenties and had dark hair, a rounded face and intense eyes, the movie actor you would try to resemble was Dick Barthelmess. So you parted your hair high on the side, increased the voltage of your eyes, wore Kollege-Kut Klothes and hoped that you looked somewhat like the Patent Leather Kid from Trinity College.

During his day there were handsomer leading men, taller, stronger and no doubt sexier, but Barthelmess, representing the slick, well-groomed, shy, sensitive, clean-cut American boy, used to draw a thousand fan letters a day.

Oddly enough, his greatest successes in that era were scored in character parts. In spite of his looks, he was a genuine actor and made a hit playing a Chinese boy opposite the lady with the most plaintive mouth on the screen—Lillian Gish. He turned up in David Wark Griffith's bucolic tear-jerker *Way Down East*, with Miss Gish as the *enceinte* heroine ordered forth into the snow with instructions never to shadow the homestead's portals again.

In 1929 the Motion Picture Academy Awards were inaugurated. An ex-Hearst reporter by the name of Adela Rogers St. John had written a script about the temptations of a young prize fighter called *The Patent Leather Kid*. This was Dick Barthelmess with his patent-leather hair, his patent-leather eyes and trim, compact body. His playing in that film won him a special Oscar for distinguished achievement.

It was curious how his life pattern followed the impression he made upon us as a young man. He retired from films, served as a lieutenant commander in the Navy in World War II and thereafter vanished from sight. But he was quietly living the life of a New York socialite—winters at 800 Park Avenue, New York, and summers on the shore at Southampton, Long Island—until in 1963 cancer silenced the pleasant voice forever.

BÉLA BARTÓK

IN the year 1928 musical America, which still accounted Debussy, Ravel and Stravinsky as "modern," caught a fleeting glimpse of the sounds of the future—that is to say, our modern idiom of today—and one of its greatest devotees.

In December of 1927 a small, shy, fragile, mild-mannered Hungarian composer by the name of Béla Bartók set foot for the first time in New York. He was sponsored by the famous Judson concert organization, and the purpose of his trip was to earn sufficient funds to rebuild his ancient Boesendorfer piano back home in Budapest.

Unknown in the United States, he turned to another Hungarian, a friend and his lifetime pupil, the pianist Erno Balogh. The Judson bureau needed photographs to familiarize the American public with their new artist. The two Hungarians went to a third Hungarian and soon found themselves in the studio of Nickolas Muray. The result was this touching study of the most misunderstood and ignored genius of his era.

The Roaring Twenties had no time for Bartók, his music or his extraordinarily far-out rhythms. The press ridiculed him, the audiences remained bewildered, cold and unappreciative.

He gave two performances of his works in New York, his Rhapsody, Opus 1, with the New York Philharmonic Orchestra conducted by Willem Mengelberg, and his Piano Concerto Number 1, involving a fourth Hungarian, Fritz Reiner, conductor of the Cincinnati Orchestra.

And that was that. The Twenties bade farewell to Bartók, neglected and underrated him. It was one of its most notable failures.

Bartók returned to the United States in 1940. In the spring of 1943 when he was desperately ill and broke, with only enough money in the house for food for a few weeks, ASCAP came to his rescue and supported him until his death in 1945. Today there is no other twentieth-century atonal composer whose output is recorded in so large a proportion.

RALPH BARTON

RALPH BARTON, cartoonist, caricaturist, satirist and illustrator, lived it up in the Twenties in New York and Paris as one of the celebrities of the time and certainly an original.

A member of the Legion of Honor of France and a full-blooded male, he used perfume and sported fancy dressing gowns. He married four times, his third wife being the actress Carlotta Monterey.

Barton didn't manage to be born with a caul, but as the next best thing he was a change-of-life baby whose mother was an artist with a studio in Kansas City. She passed her talent on directly to her son, and his first drawings were for the famous Kansas City *Star*. When he moved to New York, all doors began to open to him, and his first big hit was scored when he painted the curtain for Nikita Balieff's Russian revue, *Chauve-Souris*, caricaturing New York's notables on its huge surface.

He was famous not only for the simplicity of his line as a caricaturist, but also as a theater critic, and he was a part of the establishment of *The New Yorker* Magazine. In an interview given to Charlie Shaw for a profile of that publication in 1927, Barton made his own personal comment upon the era. He believed the then living men with the greatest influence for good to be Henry Mencken, Matisse, Toscanini, Einstein and Charlie Chaplin. Those he held to be the greatest influences for evil were Henry Ford, the Archbishop of Canterbury, Herriot, Mussolini and Stresemann.

This was his opinion of his world, and in 1931 he chose to quit it of his own volition, sitting up in bed with a cigarette in one hand, a small revolver in the other and an open copy of Gray's *Anatomy* on the counterpane. He also left his typewritten obituary, begging his friends not to speculate upon the reason for his act, but to accept his own evaluation that because he feared incipient insanity, life and work had become a torture.

In his farewell Barton wrote, "In particular, my remorse is bitter over my failure to appreciate my beautiful lost angel, Carlotta, the only woman I ever loved and whom I respect and admire above all the rest of the human race."

NORA BAYES

NOBODY in the old days ever remembered the names of songwriters. They were doomed to have the words and music they composed connected forever with the singer who first made their songs popular.

Miss Bayes, born Dora Goldberg, died in 1928 at the too young age of forty-eight, still a top star of vaudeville, musical comedy and revues. To me she is indelibly and unforgettably connected with one song—"Shine On, Harvest Moon." I can see and hear her on the stage of the old Colonial vaudeville theater at Broadway and 62nd Street, her lovely face picked out by the single spotlight. In a rich, melodious voice, she apostrophized the harvest moon in the sky, complaining lyrically of the number of months in which she had had no lovin' and hoping this same orange moon would shine upon better luck.

This was the gist of the song, but it became Nora Bayes' own. She was never let off from singing it. Often when the first bars announced it, there would be that thrill and rustle of delighted recognition through the audience, and if Miss Bayes gave us permission with the slightest gesture of encouragement, we would join in and sing it with her.

If I want to bring flooding back to me the memories of my early youth in New York—where I was, what it was like, what I was doing, who were my friends, the things we thought of and the people who were important—I have only to put on the record of Nora Bayes' "Shine On, Harvest Moon" and I am back on East 59th Street, trudging to DeWitt Clinton High School, or togged out in bell bottoms in World War I.

I never knew until recently that she was the first to sing George M. Cohan's "Over There" and that wonderful beer-garden song, "Down Where the Wurzburger Flows."

Now, almost half a century later, I can still feel the infectious gaiety of her personality, the ease and professionalism of her singing, and the way my heart vibrated in answer to her song.

DAVID BELASCO

AS the Roaring Twenties were followed by the Rueful Thirties, the greatest living legend of the American theater passed from the scene when, on May 15, 1931, David Belasco died.

In 1926, five years before his death, Muray's camera reproduced the full impact of this actor, producer, playwright, manager, Mr. Theater himself, in the image he best loved to project—the white-haired, dreamy-eyed, stunningly beautiful man of mystery in the priest's turned-around collar.

Belasco did not belong to the Twenties, but he was a fixture of the era, a vivid and dramatic part of the scene and as vital and active in the American theater as he was at the turn of the century. Then he was writing or producing such plays as *Madame Butterfly*, *The Music Master*, *The Girl of the Golden West* and *The Return of Peter Grimm*, and introducing such stars as Mrs. Leslie Carter, Blanche Bates and David Warfield.

Yet in 1928 he had three hundred actors under contract, and on the occasion of his seventy-fifth birthday he was in Atlantic City as usual, preparing to bring yet another show, *It's a Wise Child*, to New York.

Born in San Francisco of a family of Portuguese Jews, he ran away from a monastery school to join a circus and become Davido, the Boy Bare-Back Rider, the first ever to jump through a flaming hoop. In South America he fell in with a clown named Ledo, with whom he gave street shows. He was a boy actor and dramatist, played Hamlet, Marc Antony, Uncle Tom and Fagin, knew the rough mining camps of the West and the Tenderloin of New York, where he became associated with Daniel Frohman. He wore the priest's collar "in gratitude for priests who helped me to get some schooling in 'Frisco" . . . "because of the drama in me" . . . or because he felt it accentuated his natural spiritual appearance.

GEORGE BELLOWS

ONE would have had to know Jack Dempsey as I did to appreciate the manner in which George Bellows, in his famous painting of Luis Angel Firpo knocking the World Heavyweight Champion out of the ring in Jersey City, caught his likeness from the rear—the curve of his neck, the way the dark, glossy head sat upon it, and the beautiful musculature of his shoulders.

One remembers this wonderful and violent lithograph and that other famous sports painting, *Stag at Sharkey's*, which forever immortalized the brutal Frawley Law prize fights in the smoke-filled back room of some Coney Island saloon. What one tended to forget was that George Wesley Bellows was one of our finest artists, who could and often did paint with the delicacy of French Impressionists.

A nineteenth-century man—he was born in 1882 at Columbus, Ohio, growing to be six feet two and the best shortstop ever at Ohio State—Bellows was a twentieth-century painter, modern in his use of light, color and subjects, with the most tremendous zest for living, seeing and painting American life.

He broke through the barriers of what was considered "fit" for an artist to paint with his *Forty-Two Kids*, exhibited at the National Academy—nude boys in swimming. And when questioned as to whether such things lent themselves to artistic treatment, he replied, "Why not?" and went on painting the river front, the circus, stevedores on the docks and the great cliff city of New York.

When Joe Pennell criticized his *Edith Cavell* with "George would have made a better painting if he'd been on the spot," Bellows remarked that this might be true, but that he had just as good a chance to get a ticket to the execution of Edith Cavell as Leonardo had to get one for the Last Supper.

ROBERT BENCHLEY

THE first piece that Robert C. Benchley wrote was entitled "No Matter from What Angle You Looked at It, Alice Brookhansen Was a Girl Whom You Would Hesitate to Invite into Your Own Home," which title gave warning that a new humorist of the grotesque was about to appear upon the scene. But it was not until the publication in 1919, in *Vanity Fair*, of an article entitled "The Social Life of the Newt" that Bob Benchley's career as the funny man of his day was launched.

His next great contribution was a monologue, "The Treasurer's Report," in which he convulsed audiences with a straight-faced parody of a report by a confused and pompous clubman.

Bob Benchley was probably the first un-rough, un-homespun, un-grass-roots American humorist. On the contrary, a product of Worcester, Massachusetts, he was smooth, his suitings were of proper worsted, he parted his hair in the middle, prepared for college at Phillips Exeter Academy and graduated from Harvard College, where he edited and wrote for the *Harvard Lampoon*.

He filled many other roles in his lifetime, those of editor, theatrical critic and actor, but it was as a humorist that he had his impact upon the Twenties, one about whom S. J. Perelman wrote, "A good stuffy way to describe Benchley would be to say that he occupies a unique position in American humor. He occupies nothing of the sort. He is top dog."

While Will Rogers in cowboy clothes was twirling his lariat and spinning out his cracker-barrel jokes in the *Ziegfeld Follies*, Mr. Benchley in Wall Street costume was lampooning all that we held near and dear, namely ourselves.

THOMAS HART BENTON

IN that expanding decade, what Theodore Dreiser was to the novel and Eugene O'Neill to the theater, Thomas Hart Benton was to American art. And if one cared to push the analogy with the writing crafts still further, he was the Mark Twain of painters.

He is an extraordinary phenomenon, a deep-soil-rooted, backwoods American from a cultured, political family prominent in the nation's history since the days of Andrew Jackson. Benton went to Paris and was exposed to every phase of the art revolution taking place in that city at the turn of the century, from Impressionism to Fauvism to abstraction, as well as the techniques of the classicists. He rejected them all, came back to the United States, turned to America and its history for his subjects. In a different way his light composition and colors were as modern as the moderns', but in the ten years between 1920 and 1930 he found himself and a style wholly original, native and dramatic.

What was more, he was a thinking, articulate man. Plunged into a group of abstractionists back home in the United States who were working under the direction of Alfred Stieglitz the photographer, he balked and reared like a wild horse and eventually kicked his way free. Of his escape from this nonsense world he wrote: "But the idea the further you abstracted, the purer and more functionally adaptable became your forms, while logically demonstrable, wouldn't go down and stay with me."

Instead he turned to Americana—people, land, space splashed over gigantic murals. To voyage through the paintings of Tom Benton is to turn the century and pass through the decades from the rough-hewn, post-Civil War America of Indians, Negroes, pioneers of the land, through Prohibition and the new sophistication of the harsh, machine-made civilization of modern times.

HUMPHREY BOGART

THOSE who remember Humphrey Bogart—and anyone who has ever seen him has never forgotten him—recall him mostly for his later pictures: *High Sierra, Casablanca, Key Largo, The Treasure of the Sierra Madre, The African Queen, The Caine Mutiny* and *Sabrina*. These were film roles and performances that made Bogart a cult that exists to this day, although he has been dead ten years. The cultists forget that he was a highly competent stage actor on Broadway and a product of the Twenties.

A close-of-the-century baby (Christmas Day 1899), he forecast the rebel to come by being expelled from Phillips Academy at Andover, Massachusetts, for irreverence to a faculty member. Irreverence for stuffed shirts remained with him all his life.

The early Bogart who, from appearing as a stage manager for an acting group, stepped into his first roles in the early 1920's is practically unrecognizable. At the same time that Ina Claire was scoring her hit in *The Last of Mrs. Cheyney*, Mary Boland and Edna May Oliver were appearing in a comedy called *The Cradle Snatchers*. An old photograph from a scene shows an exceedingly callow youth in a dinner jacket, his hair parted dutifully in the middle, collegiate style, leaning over Miss Boland. This was Bogart. He was likewise seen in drawing-room comedies such as *Swifty, Hell's Bells* and one of the last plays to be staged by Belasco, *It's a Wise Child*. Just another of the juveniles or romantic second leads that nightly appeared in the theaters of the Gay White Way, he was getting nowhere fast.

It was not until the end of the decade that he hit somewhat the same jackpot as another smooth-haired Broadway juvenile, Edward G. Robinson. In 1934 he won the role of "Duke Mantee," a gangster who terrified a family in Robert E. Sherwood's *The Petrified Forest*. Leslie Howard was the star of the play, but it was Bogart who made it memorable, and from then on he was the tough guy of stage and film.

IRENE BORDONI

THE doughboys of 1918 sang about "Mademoiselle from Armentiers," and in the 1920's a petite, black-haired mademoiselle from Paris with dark, impish eyes and a fringe combed over her forehead appeared on Broadway to demonstrate what the soldiers had had on their minds.

Her name was Irene Bordoni, and she woke up a city emerging from innocent somnolence to the tantalizing naughtiness of her songs and personality.

She delivered the most delicious innuendoes in an accent as charmingly French as Maxim's, *midinettes* and Millet. As a matter of fact, she herself had begun life as a Paris *midinette*, one of those saucy, fresh-faced errand girls who spelled romantic enchantment for us, and she did her errands until one of them led her to the *Théâtre des Variétés*, where a director with a hole in his chorus line spotted her. At the age of thirteen, she stepped into the gap. Her talents were not conspicuous, her singing voice being unremarkable and her dancing not outstanding. But when she declaimed a slightly *risqué* song, or one that might be suspected of having a *double entendre*, her bedroom eyes and provocative little smile verified the suspicion.

And as a further matter of fact, she was actually a great-grandniece of the French painter Jean-François Millet, a print of whose famous painting *The Angelus* was to be found in practically every other American home. She taught Broadway that sex appeal and sex could be gay, lighthearted and accompanied by laughter, as opposed to the prevailing notion that it was an affair of concealment, deadly seriousness and heavy breathing. She was the very antithesis of the bosom-heaving, eye-rolling, snorting and scenery-chewing vamp who was supposed to drive strong men mad. Irene did it with a smile.

When she sang the favorites "It Must Be Love" and "Let's Do It," she created the impression that doing it was going to be the most tremendous fun.

LUCREZIA BORI

DURING those revealing Twenties the famous Metropolitan Opera House in New York welcomed the return of a singer whose lyric voice filled the auditorium and whose figure and personality conveyed illusion. She was a Mimi dying of consumption, a Manon Lescaut with whom des Grieux could be in love, and a fey and gazelle-like Mélisande.

This Spanish soprano, descendant of the famous Borgia family, was slender, graceful and exquisitely beautiful, and she came as a breath of fresh air into a theater accustomed to bovine cantatrices whose girth practically precluded the possibility of the tenor getting his arms around them during the more passionate passages.

Few divas could possibly have sung the leading role in *L'Amore dei Tre Re*, in which the script called for the basso to pick up the soprano and carry her off across his shoulder. The average female opera singer would have required a derrick. Only a little over five feet in height with lovely legs and delicate ankles, Miss Bori was easily manageable, and the stunned Metropolitan audience tendered an ovation when she was thus wafted into the wings.

As she became a fixture at the Met during the Twenties, other qualities began to dawn upon opera lovers. She was kind, generous, untemperamental, modest, gracious, courteous and magnificently courageous.

This last quality had been revealed earlier when she suddenly vanished from the scene for six years. A growth on her vocal chords had destroyed her voice. Two operations forced her into a silence that lasted for four years. Lucrezia Bori refused to believe that she would never sing again and retired to a small village in the mountains of Spain with no companion other than her Milanese maid. For two years she never spoke a single word, communicating only by gesture or with a pencil and pad. For two more years she spoke only in whispers and then, gradually retraining her voice, returned to New York for a second career, lovelier than ever.

CLARA BOW

ERIC PARTRIDGE'S *A Dictionary of Slang and Unconventional English: Colloquialisms, Vulgarisms and Such Americanisms as Have Been Naturalized* offers as its sixth interpretation of the word "It": "sexual appeal; from circa 1920." The date is right, the definition is exact, the only glaring omission is the name of the little lady responsible—Clara Bow.

Miss Bow was the first great, nationally famous, movie sex symbol, and the baby face with the tousled hair looking into the Muray camera is an indication of the sexual maturity of the Twenties. The early screen had projected "vamps" such as Theda Bara, Evelyn Nesbitt Thaw, Nita Naldi and Valeska Suratt, who were called upon to depict sex appeal as though someone had distributed itching powder inside their camisoles. Clara Bow, known as the "It Girl," ten years later was able to put over similar ideas less athletically. She was a plump little widget with fine legs, bedroom eyes, dimples, lips that were described as "bee-stung," the same being a species of fashionable baby-pout cupid's bow. She had a wild thatch of auburn hair and a come-hither wink.

She had no preparation whatsoever for the role that she was to play in our lives. Born to an ex-Coney Island waiter and a mother who was a chronic invalid and emotionally unstable, Clara quit school after eighth grade and was known in Bay Ridge as that red-haired kid on roller skates who would knock you galley-west if you got in her way. She entered and won a fan-magazine contest for beauty, and from 1925 she and "It" were with us.

Girls in those days were short-haired, light-headed dancing nymphs just beginning to proclaim their sexual emancipation. Clara Bow became Chief Vestal of the Flapper Cult. When she appeared in such pictures as *Kiss Me Again, Dancing Mothers, The Fleet's In, Man Trap*, etc., every adolescent in the audience from eight to eighty knew what "It" meant and wanted some.

The poor creature was the first of the great movie sex symbols who suffered a tragic end. She tried to live her role, survived a number of scandals, sank into mental illness and death.

ALICE BRADY

WE had fine actresses in our day and we had great troupers, and in this category Alice Brady must be listed as probably one of the best ever developed in the American theater, not only for her ability, but for her astonishing versatility.

Looking back over the years, contemporary theatrical commentators agree that no other woman had ever scored so much success in so many different mediums. For she was a star of light opera, musical comedy, straight comedy, serious drama and any role they could throw at her in motion pictures, both silent and talking. She not only sang well, but played the piano and the zither and was fluent in French, German and Italian. Her father was William A. Brady, a theatrical producer; her mother was Rose Marie René, a dancer.

Her range was incredible, from singing Gilbert and Sullivan in a sweet, high, lyric voice to playing her favorite and Academy Award-winning film part of Mrs. O'Leary in *In Old Chicago*, the Irish biddy who owned the cow whose kick supposedly started the Chicago fire.

She could produce the religious ecstasy of *The Bride of the Lamb* or the vocal tragic fury of *Mourning Becomes Electra*. She was a comedienne as well, both on the stage and in films, and it was of this comic spirit that she was most proud, claiming that she had inherited it from her Irish father and French mother.

When the Famous Players Motion Picture Company was formed, she was one of the "Big Six" actresses asked to join. She made pictures during the day and appeared on the stage at night. Among her outstanding films were *Bought and Paid For* and *The Gilded Cage*.

Not all her plays were successes; once she had a run of twelve consecutive Broadway failures. Yet she was never discouraged and never out of work. There was always a place and a role for this great trouper who could do everything and do it well. She died in 1939, at the age of forty-six.

JACK BUCHANAN

FRED ASTAIRE celebrated white tie, top hat and tails, but Jack Buchanan carried them as only an Englishman can. If he wasn't born wearing a silk hat, he acquired one shortly after.

This suave British song-and-dance man who descended upon Broadway via London in 1924, with Beatrice Lillie and Gertrude Lawrence in *Charlot's Revue*, revealed something brand new to the American theatergoing public—subtlety of British humor. He was also the best-dressed man ever seen on any stage at any time. He had a magnificent figure and his Savile Row clothes were a revelation.

Prior to the arrival of the trio from London, clowning in American musicals had been robust, frequently acrobatic and usually owed its genesis to the bladder and slapstick of the burlesque houses. Nearly all of America's great comics had served an apprenticeship at one time or another in burleycue.

Jack Buchanan was an intellectual comedian, master of the elevated eyebrow, the rueful smile or the satirical grimace. He made his points as well by the merest inflections of the most cultured British accent to be heard on the Great White Way.

Each of the three brilliant stars who burst like fireworks from *Charlot's Revue* and the show itself made a permanent impact on the concept of musical entertainment in America. Buchanan's contribution was the discovery that laughter could be combined with style, fastidiousness and charm. Strikingly handsome, an easy, graceful dancer, with his every appearance he provided an object lesson in fluency, polish and good taste. American audiences loved him.

From then on Buchanan was never long away from Broadway, solidifying his early impression upon us with further editions of *Charlot's Revue* and musicals such as *Wake Up and Dream*, and continued as a perennial favorite in films and TV as well as the stage until his death in 1957.

BILLIE BURKE

THIS misty-eyed, luminous beauty attracted the attentions of connoisseurs of the pre-Twenties era from Enrico Caruso, who hopefully dispatched large quantities of flowers to her dressing room, to Willie Maugham, who took her dancing. Signor Caruso's objective was marriage, but Miss Burke recalls that at that time she didn't care to have her career cluttered with matrimony. And she went dancing with Mr. Maugham because she was appearing in one of his plays and the British author was pleased to be seen with this sensitive beauty with the blue eyes and red-gold hair.

But the man she married (encountered at one of the dances) was Florenz Ziegfeld, who himself earmarked the decade between 1920 and 1930 with his *Follies* "glorifying" the American girl.

If you will study the portrait of Miss Burke, you will see what it was that came through onto Muray's sensitized plate—a dear, good person—and she was as beloved on Broadway for herself, her cheerfulness and kindness, as for her skill in the roles she portrayed.

Her father, William Burke, was a circus clown, and the daughter who was named Mary William Ethelbert Appleton inherited the sharp humor of the Big Top, which in her was turned into a delicious flare for the ludicrous.

In the Twenties she appeared in *Intimate Strangers* and *Rose Briar*, sang her way through *Annie Dear* and played the title role in Noel Coward's *The Marquise*. She scored in *The Happy Husband* and *Family Affairs*, and closed out the decade with *The Truth Game*.

But it was as wife to the legendary Florenz Ziegfeld that she fitted into the scene of those years. As wife and mother she coped with a difficult and temperamental husband, was a witty and graceful hostess who knew everyone in New York worth knowing, and, by being herself, indelibly placed the stamp of her personality upon the era.

SIR HALL CAINE

NO one could accuse Sir Hall Caine of being a child of the Twenties, or even a favorite of that era, but certainly he shared in our general awakening from literary somnolence and in particular our discovery of foreign lions of letters.

No little credit for this awareness was due to Muray's journey abroad with his big studio camera and tripod to photograph ten famous people, including Sir Hall Caine.

Arriving at Sir Hall's home for the appointment, Muray quickly unendeared himself to his wife by addressing her as Lady Hall. This apparently upset and angered Lady Caine, as she should have been addressed, and she left Muray to find his own way upstairs, where Sir Hall, then a spry seventy-three, roared with laughter and in a few moments the Pre-Raphaelite novelist and the Greenwich Village photographer were the best of friends. Sir Hall himself posed the shot of how he did his writing, pad on lap and usually seated in a chair inherited from Dante Gabriel Rossetti, the poet-painter with whom he had lived for six years until Rossetti died in his arms.

His own era was that of Victoria; the setting of most of his plays and novels, the Isle of Man, where he was born. But it was after the First World War that he achieved his greatest popularity in the United States with *The Deemster*, *The Manxman*, *The Christian* and *The Eternal City*, although they were all written before 1901. With the advent of moving pictures he wrote a highly successful film, *Darby and Joan*.

New Yorkers had also encountered his byline in *The New York Times* during the war, at which time he had served as a correspondent for the paper, disseminating both news and British propaganda, for which he was knighted by King George V in 1918.

He laid down his pen for the last time on August 31, 1931.

IRENE CASTLE

IN the last days of the silent pictures, just before the talkies, a leading lady who used to play opposite such stars as Elliot Dexter, Milton Sills and Rod La Rocque was nearly drowned when the script called for her to dive off a fifty-foot rock into the open sea at Marblehead, Massachusetts. She surfaced to discover that they had neglected to provide a boat for her in which to get ashore. It was touch-and-go before a human chain finally pulled her out of the raging tide, badly cut by barnacles.

Another time she was directed to swim with a child on her back and was nearly killed on that occasion too. And, believe it or not, in yet another film she filled up with water trying to hold up leading man Dexter when it developed, somewhat belatedly, as he was shoved off the deep end, that he couldn't swim.

Who was this water Naiad who performed her own swimming stunts? Gertrude Ederle? Esther Williams? Not a bit of it. She was an ex-professional ballroom dancer who a decade before had changed the faces and forms and clothes of women, and made young and old America dance-conscious. Her name was Irene Castle.

Prior to the advent of Irene and her husband Vernon Castle upon the scene, Americans were indulging in dance-floor grotesqueries known as the Turkey Trot and the Bunny Hug. The smooth Castles introduced graceful, flowing movements and became a sensation.

Irene cut her hair short (the hairpins were always falling out) and the Irene Castle bob became all the rage. She had always been slim-hipped, flat-chested. Women all over the country began queuing up at reducing establishments. And the clothes she wore to outline the long, slender lines of her body as well as to emphasize the movements of her dancing became the fashion, even to the Irene Castle bonnet, with which she posed for Nick Muray's *Vanity Fair* study of her.

WILLA CATHER

IF you had wandered the streets of New York's Bohemia in the early Twenties, you would have passed by the houses of three of our greatest home-bred novelists who were sharing in the literary renaissance, an outpouring of fiction that was to give a new impetus to American writing. On St. Luke's Place lived Theodore Dreiser; in the house next door Sherwood Anderson rented a floor; and at No. 5 Bank Street, one of the quietest and pleasantest streets of the northwestern Village, dwelt a serious, solitary woman novelist, Willa Cather.

It was natural that this mistress of letters should at some time sit for the Village photographer whose portrait studies of the painters, writers, sculptors and theatrical celebrities who inhabited this old New York enclave in the heart of the modern city were already making him famous.

There were literary giantesses then, as well as giants—novelists of the magnitude of Edith Wharton, Ellen Glasgow, Susan Glaspell, Edna Ferber, Fannie Hurst and Djuna Barnes, and poetesses such as Edna St. Vincent Millay and Elinor Wylie. Miss Cather stood tall and proud amongst them.

Books were read in those days for reading's sake rather than as an aphrodisiac or a nerve shock to jaded, flagging sexual appetites. The present generation hardly reads Willa Cather's deeply understanding, charmingly written novels, but those of us who did find memories lingering.

Some of the sadness inspired by *A Lost Lady* and the tragic disintegration of Marian Forrester still remains. Who could forget the quiet, sincere strength of Antonia in *My Antonia*, or the New Mexican saga of Bishop Jean Latour and Father Joseph Vaillant in their battle for the souls of the Hopi and Navajo Indians in *Death Comes for the Archbishop*?

In 1922 her novel *One of Ours* won the Pulitzer Prize.

FEODOR CHALIAPIN

NEW YORK had never seen anyone like him before, nor any such performance on an operatic stage as Feodor Chaliapin's interpretation of the mad Russian Czar in *Boris Godounoff*. Until the advent of this six-foot-four-inch, blond, blue-eyed *basso profundo*, grand opera was an entertainment for a highly specialized audience of genuine music lovers on the one hand and society people on the other, both of whom suffered through renditions by performers who, though magnificent singers, were probably the worst actors in the world.

Chaliapin changed all this, at least for any role in which he appeared at the Met in the early Twenties. From the moment he appeared upon the great stage through the mad scene of the Czar, which he tore to tatters, a thrill ran through the jaded ranks of socialites and bespectacled intellectuals, who suddenly realized that they were not only listening to the greatest bass of the century, but were witnessing the most tremendous dramatic stage performance of the season as well.

New York had to grow up to Chaliapin, for during his first visit, in 1907, this gargantuan fellow whose life was as *bravura* as his performances was too rough for the Nice Nelly critics of that day. They complained of his bestiality incarnate when he entered as Mephistopheles stripped to the waist with the upper half of his body covered with luminous paint, and his disgusting frankness when, as Don Basilio in *The Barber of Seville*, he wiped his nose on the sleeve of his cassock.

Born in Kazan, his father a drunkard, he was apprenticed to a cobbler in the same street where Maxim Gorki was working in a baker's cellar. At the age of seventeen he joined a traveling troupe, but not before he had been a wood-carver, a bookbinder, a pawnbroker's clerk, a novice in a monastery and a longshoreman on the Volga.

CHARLES SPENCER CHAPLIN

THIS handsome young man with the introspective eyes, when equipped with a toothbrush mustache, bowler hat, baggy trousers, slap shoes, a shuffling walk and a bamboo cane, was responsible for reducing moving-picture audiences into such a state that often the very building appeared to sway and rock as people lost all control of their risibilities, howled, whooped, shrieked, shouted and guffawed.

Since the days when Charlie Chaplin made his first full-length picture, *Tilly's Punctured Romance* with Marie Dressler, and progressed through *A Dog's Life, Shoulder Arms, The Kid, The Idle Class, The Gold Rush, The Circus* and others, and his retirement from the character of the little tramp, no such gusts, gales or cyclones of amusement have blown through any theater. To have lived and laughed in the era of Chaplin's prime is to partake of memories that are unique and unmatched.

Of this sitting Muray wrote, "Like most professional entertainers, particularly comedians, he loved to hold the center of the stage and it was no hardship to get him in the mood for posing, although several times I asked him to cut out the funny quips and let me try to make something from within, rather than just show the 'front.' I had some records in the studio which I borrowed from Vladimir Horowitz the pianist, a mutual friend, and we began discussing serious music. I got several pictures where his inner character, usually hidden by his comic artistry, came through."

There was always that touch of sadness in the Chaplin humor, inherited from the days of his childhood with his father dead from drink when the boy was five and his mother alternating between mental breakdowns, the poorhouse and squalid hovels in London's East End.

The man in the photo was already a millionaire, but behind the eyes the memories linger.

INA CLAIRE

WHILE the more juvenile characters of our times were flipping for flappers and elevating the petulant cupid's-bow pout to the national erotic symbol, more adult and cultivated theatergoers were eyeing with delight one of the smartest and loveliest women to appear upon the theatrical scene. This was an Irish girl with blond hair, blue eyes and an Irish sense of humor that illuminated every lineament of her face. Born Ina Fagan in Washington, D.C., for her stage name she chose Ina Claire. She was the most brilliant light comedienne of her time, endowed with grace of movement, perfect diction, faultless timing, flashing wit and a complete relaxation while on stage.

Her forte was sophisticated drawing-room comedy, and her most famous plays of the 1920's were *Bluebeard's Eighth Wife*, *The Awful Truth*, *Grounds for Divorce*, *Our Betters* and her biggest hit, *The Last of Mrs. Cheyney*. She moved through these comedies poised, elegant and sparkling.

Many years later George Sidney, the Hollywood director, was to say of her, "Of all the actresses I have ever known, there was none who could deliver a line with the quiet, devastating timing of Ina Claire." Her feeling for the theater was such that when the playwright S. N. Behrman's sense of dramatic structure failed him, as it sometimes did, Ina would bring him back onto the track simply by standing in the center of the rehearsal stage, looking him squarely in the eyes and saying, "Sam, this play is about me, isn't it? So what do I do next?" Miss Claire managed to make all plays in which she acted appear to be about her.

Capable, volatile and youthful-appearing, the actress now decorates the city of San Francisco, where she lives with her lawyer husband, William Wallace.

JEAN COCTEAU

WHAT did they look like when they were young, these geniuses of another century who survived to die in the arms of today? The camera obscura is there to tell us the story.

When Jean Cocteau quit the scene he had decorated for more than half a century in 1963, he was so thin and wasted by the furious fires of creation that consumed him that someone said he looked like two profiles stuck together. There was very little left of him. But here is the young man who was a poet, playwright, critic, painter, book illustrator, decorator, designer, muralist and producer-director for stage and screen, as he appeared in the mid-Twenties. Then, commuting back and forth between New York and his native Paris, and because of grief at the death of a friend and protégé, the novelist Raymond Radiguet, he took first to opium and later to conversion to Roman Catholicism.

This studious-looking French boy with the strange dimple beneath the generous nose was a continuously exploding box of fireworks who had a fling at every ism erupting early in the Parisian twentieth century: cubism, dada-ism, surrealism. He wrote ballets, oratorios, novels, poems, farces, monologues, tragedies. His pen, pencil and palette were so far out in advance that we never did quite catch up to him.

As a lecturer he surprised and shocked American college girls with his frank and unorthodox approach to the great gods Corneille and Racine, whom he up-ended. He joined forces with every great artistic revolutionary: Diaghilev, Picasso, Darius Milhaud, Stravinsky, Honegger and Hindemith were his collaborators. He antedated the non-films of today by thirty years with *The Blood of a Poet*, a piece in which fact and dreams mingled and which nobody could understand. He evolved ideas for ballet and designs for evening frocks and neckties for Schiaparelli, played traps in a night club and typified what every young artist craved to be, a nonconformist genius on the loose.

CLAUDETTE COLBERT

IN those exciting Twenties, Broadway was the incubator for the great motion-picture stars of the Thirties and the Forties, young actors and actresses who appeared briefly and often unsensationally in Broadway productions. In that era some 250 shows a year actually opened on the Great White Way, many kept alive by cut-rate theater-ticket agencies which sold you a $2 ticket for $1.10, whereas today a play survives because of the enormous "buys" of scalper agencies who invest in a play and sell you a $10 ticket for $25.

The theater was healthy, and Hollywood reached down to lease some of its lesser lights such as Spencer Tracy, Barbara Stanwyck, Miriam Hopkins, Archie Leach (who became better known as Cary Grant), Clark Gable and Claudette Colbert. This last pair was to achieve stardom and Oscardom in the "screamies" in that most daring and enchanting comedy, *It Happened One Night*.

Although, like so many actresses before and after her, Miss Colbert came a cropper in the role of Cleopatra, she was never far away from camera and microphone and her role as one of the darlings of the American talkies with her fresh, heart-shaped face and ravishing legs.

But who was Claudette Colbert? And how did she get there?

She was born in Paris as Lili Chauchoin, emigrated to America at the age of thirteen with her parents and rounded out her education at Washington Irving High School near Union Square in New York. That French *quelque chose* grafted to American brass and the ability to tell fanciful stories about her talents saw her through a number of producers' offices, some early plays and some terrible notices. At last, by trial and error coupled with native charm, in 1927 she appeared on Broadway in a play called *The Barker* and Hollywood sat up and noticed.

JACKIE COOGAN

JACKIE COOGAN was four years old when he began to make *The Kid*, five when the picture was released; two hours later he was on his way to becoming a world celebrity. He was the first of the great child actors. A little girl by the name of Shirley Temple was the second, unless one counts that early infant of the Hal Roach *Our Gang* comedies, Baby Peggy.

Sudden fame, of course, was one of the hallmarks of the Twenties and in particular of the developing art of the black-and-white pictures that moved. Wealth showered upon individuals who never before had had two pennies to press together, and celebrity upon steppers or song-and-dance men who had never been more than third-rate vaudevillians.

Jackie was born in a theatrical trunk. His father, Jack, was a four-a-day hoofer; his mother, Lilian, herself a onetime child actress. When Jackie was just four, his father was dancing in an act at the Los Angeles Orpheum featuring Annette Kellerman, the one-piece-bathing-suit swimmer. One evening Miss Kellerman called the baby from the wings onto the stage, where he did a version of the "Shimmy" (then the dance craze of America) and brought the house down. He became a part of the act, and a week later Chaplin saw him and interviewed the Coogans.

"Can he cry?" Chaplin asked. "Cry!" said Daddy Coogan. Jackie cried. "Can he do it again?" Chaplin asked. Jackie did. *The Kid* was on the way.

Three years later the Coogans were millionaires and lived in a mansion with three Rolls Royces. And wherever Jackie appeared, at home or abroad, mobs formed to try to get near enough to touch him.

This is the face of the child who in six years of films earned eight million dollars by stirring the heart of a generation.

CALVIN COOLIDGE

ONE of the paradoxes of our time was that during six years of America's high-living, hard-drinking, loose-moraled, money-making, postwar holiday spree, the nation was governed from the White House by a dour, sour-faced New England President, a Vermonter of Puritan stock descended from a long line of New England farmers and storekeepers, a man of unimpeachable honesty, selfless courage and practically nonexisting speech. The face of Calvin Coolidge tells the story: no humor, no nonsense, absolute integrity and plenty of common sense. He was a President greatly beloved and respected by his countrymen, perhaps because while all of us were losing our heads slightly in one way or another, he was keeping his, holding the nation on an even keel, protecting its prosperity and letting us make fools of ourselves while he minded the store.

Nick Muray wanted to unfreeze the President if he could. Mr. Coolidge won. Here are Muray's notes on the meeting:

"A sitting with 'Silent Cal' presented a challenge—what could one do with the Great Stone Face? I was only allotted ten minutes, and, as you can imagine, I set up very carefully to ensure results. As I was placing the lights I could hear from an adjoining room a great commotion, bumps and crashes as if furniture were being moved. The aide who was functioning as stand-in explained that the President was playing with his dogs. I figured that any animal-lover could be softened into a smile, and planned my strategy accordingly.

"Promptly at the designated moment, Coolidge entered. A quick introduction, and he was in front of the camera. Since I knew exactly what I wanted, I worked very fast, and had the necessary negatives in short order. Then I said, 'Mr. President, it's only eight minutes, but I'm finished,' hoping for and ready for the smile I was so sure would come. Not at all. The President mumbled, 'Thanks!' and left."

GRACE GOODHUE COOLIDGE

SHE was probably one of the least noticeable and unostentatious of the wives of our Presidents, but we gradually became aware that from 1923 to 1929 there was a genuine lady occupying the White House, a woman of simplicity, femininity and dignity. She radiated a sweetness and warmth of manner which went far to counteract the stiff, cold, un-outgoing personality of her husband, President Calvin Coolidge.

Daughter of a Vermont deacon and government steamboat inspector, graduate of Vermont University, she was equal to any occasion, and where her monosyllabic husband repelled, she made friends. Whether she was receiving Queen Marie of Rumania, the first reigning sovereign ever to be welcomed officially in the United States, or David Windsor, Prince of Wales, or Charles Lindbergh, or the wives of Senators and Congressmen, or glad-handers from the home state, she was her simple, graceful self who did honor to the title of the First Lady of the Land.

She was steadfastly at her husband's side, and her presence was of no little importance to his rise from Mayor to State Senator, Lieutenant Governor, Governor of Massachusetts and eventually President of the United States. It was not until Coolidge assumed the governorship and moved to the executive mansion in Boston that their scale of living for the first time included such luxury as a family automobile.

One might turn to Grace Coolidge to remember that while the rout and carnival of the Twenties was enlivening New York and other cities like a perpetual Mardi Gras, this was not true of the country at large. The major part of America was living and toiling with the same quiet sincerity as the wife of the President.

KATHARINE CORNELL

IN 1917 that incubator of stars of the Twenties, the Washington Square Players, produced Andreyev's play *The Life of Man*, which begins with the agonized screams of an off-stage mother bearing a child, and Lawrence Langner in his book *The Magic Curtain* recounts that various mothers who were tested for the role could barely be heard beyond the third row of the orchestra. Finally a young girl recently introduced and on the fringe of the company was given an audition and, though neither wife nor mother, she produced such blood-curdling shrieks that she got the part. And when the curtain rose on the first performance, so appalling were her screams that two frightened old ladies in the front row of the orchestra fled the theater. The name of the screamer was Miss Katharine Cornell.

Ten years later the off-stage yell was being called the First Lady of the American Theater, a title disputed only by that *enfant terrible* of the critics, George Jean Nathan. Touting Miss Margaret Anglin for that honor, he disparaged not only Miss Cornell's performance but the plays in which she appeared as well. He referred to such popular opuses of the decade as *The Green Hat, Nice People, Dishonored Lady* as "things"; *The Enchanted Cottage* as a "dish of mush"; *The Outsider* as "a geyser of hocum"; and *Casanova* as "a *couturier's* party." He was compelled to admit that she gave an intelligent and lovely performance in *Candida* and an even more intelligent and lovelier performance in *The Barretts of Wimpole Street*.

Mr. Nathan's critical sniffs were not shared by the theatergoers. For us Miss Cornell presented nightly the same wistful, sensitive enchantment she brought later to the role of Juliet—the first Juliet I can remember who made me believe.

MIGUEL COVARRUBIAS

IN 1957 in Mexico City the body of a great artist-anthropologist, dead at fifty-three, lay in state in the National Museum of Anthropology and History. It was difficult to equate the author of a historical study of the Olmec Indians of Tehuantepec and Professor of the History of Art at the National Anthropological School of Mexico with the bubbling, antic, irresponsible, nineteen-year-old caricaturist who arrived in New York in 1923 to study art on a grant from the Mexican government.

It didn't take him long to discover Greenwich Village and a bosom pal in photographer Muray. Art school went by the board, and the laughing Miguel was a part of the burgeoning New York artists' and writers' colony that included Carl Van Vechten, Ralph Barton, James Weldon Johnson, Arthur Machen, Jo Davidson, Carl Van Doren, Noel Coward and Henry Mencken.

In no time at all Miguel ran through his fellowship funds. It was Frank Crowninshield, editor of *Vanity Fair*, who came to his rescue by publishing his caricatures and the famous series known as "Impossible Interviews," such as meetings between Rockefeller Senior and Stalin, Garbo and Calvin Coolidge.

Even more trenchant, however, were Covarrubias' ventures into Harlem, where his palette and brush were doing for the Negroes of that ghetto what Van Vechten's prose was accomplishing at the same time, revealing that other world—the dark-skinned city, north of 125th Street, within a light-skinned city. It was during the Twenties that Harlem was "discovered" and slumming parties used to take cabs northward after midnight to the Cotton Club. Already the makings of Señor Covarrubias the mature anthropologist were there as he caught and exposed the essential nature of the Harlemites of those days.

NOEL COWARD

AMONG the number of illusions dispelled or abandoned as America came of age was the notion that the Englishman was a dense and humorless fellow. Americans had been limited to a diet of travesty Britishers, caricatures as broad and misleading as the "Waaal I swan" American hayseed farmer or the burlesque-house Jew.

American doughboys returning from France at the end of World War I had rather a different idea. They had fought alongside the wry British Tommy in the trenches, and laughed at the cartoons of Bruce Bairnsfather.

And then, of course, there was Noel Coward.

Coward is so contemporary today, so much "with us" as well as "with it" with his plays, novels, short stories, songs and poetry, his satyr's face and ubiquitous appearances in London, Paris, New York, Hollywood, on stage or film set, that we tend to forget that he was a phenomenon of the Twenties.

He is Jack and Master of all trades in the theater: playwright, actor, director, lyricist and composer. His songs are unforgettable and a permanent part of light musical literature; his plays stand the test of time and are as entertaining in 1967 as they were in the Twenties, when he wrote such successes as *Hay Fever*, *Fallen Angels*, *The Vortex*, *Easy Virtue*, *This Year of Grace*, *Bitter Sweet* and *Private Lives*.

He was the Messrs. Gilbert and Sullivan combined, since he wrote the book, the words and the music all himself. He was at home in any medium of entertainment, ranging from vaudeville and cabaret in his young days to defying the prying eye of television of modern times, and he was equally facile at writing and directing films. He can produce short stories and novels.

Born into a middle-class family of the Teddington district of London, he has scored the remarkable achievement of turning himself into the symbol of the highest British upper stratum, Oxford-Etonian sophistication.

JANE COWL

IT would seem that forty years ago Broadway's cornucopia of stars and great actresses was bottomless. Actresses of the caliber of Jane Cowl, Florence Reed, Lenore Ulric, Alice Brady, Helen Hayes, Eva Le Gallienne, Jeanne Eagels headed an endless list of exquisite women who, no matter what they touched, could fill the theater with magic. Jane Cowl was not only one of the most talented of these actresses, but a playwright as well who wrote and played in such long-running hits as *Lilac Time* and *Smilin' Through*. She was a famous Juliet and, with Rollo Peters as Romeo, racked up one of Will Shakespeare's longest Broadway runs, playing the role for 157 performances beginning in December 1922 at Henry Miller's Theatre. Then she took the show on the road and continued for 682 appearances.

At her last New York performance in this role, 2,000 persons were turned away at the box office and 3,000 gathered in the streets outside the theater to say goodbye to the actress whom one critic termed the most beautiful woman on the American stage. And this in a day when there were such exquisite creatures as Helen Gahagan, Selena Royle, Miriam Hopkins, Pauline Lord and Blanche Yurka to offer competition in the beauty stakes.

She was a woman's actress and a matinee idol who was sometimes referred to as "Jane Howl," from the ease with which she was able to open her tear ducts and the roles which called for her to spend much of her time weeping. She was equally at home in such modern tear-jerkers as *The Depths* and Noel Coward's *Easy Virtue* as in costume dramas such as *Pelléas and Mélisande, Antony and Cleopatra, Paolo and Francesca* and *Twelfth Night*. There was not a year of that decade from 1920 to 1930 when Jane Cowl was not lighting up a Broadway stage.

JOAN CRAWFORD AND DOUGLAS FAIRBANKS, JR.

THE lovely girl herewith is a member of the Board of Directors of one of the world's major corporations, the Pepsi-Cola Company. The boy is a Knight Commander of the Order of the British Empire, a captain in the United States Naval Reserve and the holder of as many medals and decorations (twenty-two, to be exact) as a crowned head. But when Muray trained his camera upon this young married couple by the seaside, they stood for glamour: Joan Crawford (born Lucille Le Sueur) and Douglas Fairbanks, Jr., motion-picture stars.

It was in our dizzy Twenties that the word "glamour" first came loose from the pages of Webster to be a part of our everyday thought and spoken language. The definitions offered are: "Enchantment; any interest in or association with an object or person through which the object or person appears delusively magnified or glorified; to affect with glamour, to bewitch, fascinate, enchant."

All of this applied to Joan Crawford, with the exception that there was nothing delusive about her enchantment. She was the one moving-picture queen who was consistently glamorous off the screen as well as on.

Douglas Fairbanks, Jr., successful son of the famous father, was educated in American military academies as well as in London and Paris, and in 1927 was playing in *Young Woodley* at the Pasadena Playhouse. Paul Bern of Jean Harlow fame took Joan Crawford to see the play and then backstage. In the middle of the night Joan picked up the phone and sent Douglas a congratulatory telegram. They met again and flared up like magnesium. That the marriage didn't last was symptomatic of the era.

Although we didn't know it at the time, Joan Crawford was the first of the picture stars endowed with intelligence which led her to study her profession—not only acting before the camera, but the function of the camera itself. Today, at the age of fifty-nine, she can help run a business, mother four adopted children and still, when the spirit moves her, revive her glamour in films or television.

FRANK CROWNINSHIELD

THIS delicious man was one of the prime cultural gadflies of the Twenties. Webster defines the adjective as "affording exquisite pleasure or entertainment," and during his tenure of the editorship of *Vanity Fair* the late Francis Welch Crowninshield did just that.

Born in Paris, June 24, 1873, to an American artist father, Crownie was the embodiment of Old World courtesy, youthful verve, impishness, kindness, generosity, wit, talent and prescience. In short, he was to the day of his death one of the most wholly lovable and delightful men of times past and present.

A character usually referred to as "the last of the gentlemen of the old school," bachelor, *bon vivant*, a man of breeding and exquisite manners with an avuncular eye for fluffy young things, he was also a most modern man, a pioneer and a stick of dynamite. A connoisseur and *avant-gardist* of impeccable taste, his judgments of young artists, writers and musicians launched in the Twenties were verified when they became the giants of the Forties, Fifties and Sixties. He was one of the organizers of the first great Armory show of French Impressionists as far back as 1913.

For a sweet old gentleman, he could be exceedingly naughty and biting, as when he created the "We Nominate for Oblivion—" department in *Vanity Fair*, to sting public bores and phonies.

He was the first to publish Gertrude Stein in the U.S. He gave page room to André Gide, Compton Mackenzie and D. H. Lawrence, and presented Aldous Huxley, Hugh Walpole and Somerset Maugham.

It was Crownie who paid the first dollar ever earned in America to a then unknown young British actor by the name of Noel Coward, for a satirical article. Dorothy Parker, Bob Benchley and Robert Sherwood were his discoveries. He published Edna St. Vincent Millay, Elinor Wylie, P. G. Wodehouse, as well as Thomas Wolfe, E. E. Cummings, Colette, Molnár, Edmund Wilson, Corey Ford and Gilbert Seldes.

At the same time he was illuminating his magazine with full-color reproductions of paintings by Renoir, Picasso, Matisse, Rouault, Gauguin, Segonzac, Van Gogh, Braque, Modigliani and Chirico, as well as sculpture by Epstein, Manship, Despiau, Davidson and Whitney.

The "sweet old gentleman" was providing the startled Twenties with a rousing and authentic preview of modern times.

BEBE DANIELS

THE ten years from 1920 to 1930, give and take a few on either side, might be designated as the greatest producers and developers of talent in the history of the American performing arts. For this was a time of extraordinary opportunity for young talent in every walk of life.

Who would have imagined that a baby girl born in Dallas, Texas, on January 14, 1901, of Scottish-Spanish show-business parents, would in twenty years see her name a household word, in forty find herself reigning as an international star of films, plays, musical comedies and radio, and with her husband, Ben Lyon, beloved on both sides of the Atlantic, and a London wartime heroine to boot? This was, and still is, Bebe Daniels.

She was named Bebe—Spanish for "baby," but it was never pronounced anything other than "Bee-Bee." She made her stage debut as a Shakespearean actress at the age of four when she toured the country as one of the little Princes in the Tower in *Richard III*. She starred in some seventy-five moving pictures during her career, not counting the two hundred or so comedies she made as leading lady to Harold Lloyd and Snub Pollard.

For, naturally talented as she was, Bebe Daniels was particularly fortunate in falling into slapstick comedy.

The magnitude of Charles Chaplin sometimes makes us forget that there were other great screen clowns contemporary with him: Buster Keaton, Harold Lloyd, Laurel and Hardy and a host of lesser zanies. These had to have leading ladies, and the leading ladies had to play it straight. There is no art more difficult than to feed laughs to a clown and yet maintain sympathy and sex appeal.

As Harold Lloyd's leading lady, Bebe Daniels averaged a comedy a week, and after a while there was nothing she couldn't do. When Cecil B. DeMille saw her in a restaurant and offered her her first dramatic role, she was ready.

CLARENCE DARROW

CLARENCE SEWARD DARROW was a lawyer for the defense. He was the most famous legal light of the mid-Twenties and within the span of two years, 1924 and 1925, achieved three victories for the defense that made him world famous. In the face of bitter racist feeling, he secured the acquittal of a Negro in Chicago who shot and killed a white man, one of a mob attacking the home of a Negro doctor. This success marked an early step in the campaign for civil rights.

He defended Leopold and Loeb, two rich Chicago boys who produced the first example of what today has become almost an accepted part of our way of life—the motiveless, psychopathic murder. Darrow cheated the gallows and got them life imprisonment because he was a lifelong hater of capital punishment, which he regarded as legalized murder.

And he defended the liberties of the rational thinker against the hidebound bigot in the most famous of all his cases and certainly the most sensational legal battle of the decade. This was the Scopes trial, when Darrow, an atheist and agnostic, invaded the Bible Belt of the South and at Dayton, Tennessee, defended schoolteacher John T. Scopes for teaching Darwinian evolution in the public school there. His opponent for the prosecution in this dramatic case was fundamentalist William Jennings Bryan, who was compelled to take the witness stand and declare in open court that he believed the mythological, symbolical, Hebraic text of the Bible word for word. More than any single person, Darrow awakened America and Americans to the discoveries of science and the origin of man.

Darrow embodied in his own personal life and behavior every virtue preached but not always practiced by the so-called Christians: love and pity for his fellow man, humility, generosity, unselfishness, honesty, humanitarianism and deep-rooted kindness. Physically, Muray described him as "a noble human sculpture."

MARLENE DIETRICH

SHE is a woman of the ages, but a child of the Twenties. A melancholy blonde-pigtailed school-girl in the starving Germany of World War I, a nervous, ambitious bit player during the next decade, Marlene Dietrich was to startle the entertainment world in *The Blue Angel.*

She was not a pretty child, she remembers—the great, glamorous stage beauties of maturity rarely were—and no one ever thought about her legs when, as a teenager, she dutifully took piano and violin lessons from the local teacher to the point where she could have become a professional concert artist on either instrument.

Her father was killed in the war; she lived with her mother, grandmother and sister in a Germanic home where rules and regulations were the order of the day, and their strictness forced her into the retirement of dreams.

She became a linguist and a scholar until she was swept up in the Reich's postwar turmoil and breakdown. Marlene became stagestruck.

The ugly duckling had grown into a beautiful, slender woman with a curiously deep and un-melodious voice. She admits that her talents were limited. She has most poignant memories of the early days of struggle when she joined Max Reinhardt's repertory company as a bit player, and her parts *were* bits. She recalls a dress she wore in one scene—chiffon in two shades of gray with sequins and bugle beads and lovely embroidery down the back, but the front consisted of nothing but a panel of dressmaker's lining. The young actress was appalled at the half-costume.

"That's all right," she was told. "You're seated at a bridge table with your back to the audience, and you don't turn around."

Her one line in the play was, "Pass!" and nobody ever heard her say it.

RUTH DRAPER

AMONGST the other startling phenomena of an era that was exploding like a nova, theater-goers discovered that there was genuinely something new under the sun. It was a young woman who came upon a stage bare of all scenery beyond a table and a chair. She wore no costumes other than an occasional change of hat or shawl or a coat over a plain brown dress, and she never varied her make-up from one characterization to another.

Within a few minutes, when she had launched into one of her thirty-six original monologues, the stage was set with imaginary scenery, anything that Ruth Draper wished her audience to see, and peopled with from one to half a dozen characters simultaneously, all played or induced by Miss Draper alone. She had some fifty-seven of these from which to choose. She was a one-woman show, a one-woman evening and, actually, a one-woman theater. When she died in 1956 at the age of seventy-two, she was world famous, had received honorary degrees from universities in the United States and Great Britain, had given a command performance at Windsor Castle and been made a Commander of the Order of the British Empire.

She was the daughter of Dr. William H. and Ruth Dana Draper of New York City and the granddaughter of Charles A. Dana, the famous editor of the New York *Sun*. She was educated privately and at an early age began to entertain friends and elders with her skill at mimicry. Soon she was giving performances at schools and for charities. As an indication of the circles in which this extraordinary girl moved, it was none other than Ignace Jan Paderewski, the pianist and Polish statesman, who persuaded her to become a professional actress.

JEANNE EAGELS

THE year 1922 was another standout on Broadway. *Abie's Irish Rose* was born, destined to run for 2,327 performances; John Barrymore broke records in his production of *Hamlet;* and for the first time the movies were satirized in *Merton of the Movies* with Glenn Hunter.

To old-timers the names of plays and players that opened on the Street that year will ring like bells: *Seventh Heaven* with Helen Menken, *He Who Gets Slapped* with Richard Bennett and Margalo Gillmore, *The Torch Bearers* with Mary Boland and Alison Skipworth. Louis Wolheim played *The Hairy Ape*, and Frances Starr, Ina Claire, Helen Hayes, Florence Reed and Marjorie Rambeau were all seen in new plays.

Yet even in such a year there was one star that topped them all—a girl who came on stage wearing an ostrich-feather hat, tassel scarf, lace shawl, white clocked socks and high button shoes, carrying an umbrella and an air of defiance. The name of the actress was Jeanne Eagels and the character she played was Sadie Thompson, prostitute. The play was *Rain*, adapted by John Colton in collaboration with Clemence Randolph from the short story "Miss Thompson" by Somerset Maugham.

Miss Eagels stood New York on its ears with her portrayal of Mr. Maugham's professional lady.

An ex-chorus girl who fought her way to the top of the ladder, Jeanne Eagels became one of the characters of the decade through her frantic romance with the boss of the waterfront stevedores. She made headlines when, during a shipboard quarrel, he tore from her neck the diamond necklace with which he had presented her and tossed it overboard. Her first real hit was under the egis of David Belasco in *Daddies*, in 1918; her last with Leslie Howard in 1927, in *Her Cardboard Lover*.

On October 9, 1929, in New York, the city toxicologist announced his findings on Jeanne Eagels, motion-picture and stage star, who died at the Park Avenue Hospital: death from an overdose of chloral hydrate.

MISCHA ELMAN

THERE was no dearth of violinists in our times. There was no lack of outstanding artists in any field, for that matter. One of the most brilliant was Mischa Elman, Russian-born concert artist who became a naturalized American citizen in mid-decade—i.e., 1925. He was so well known and so much a part of the American concert scene that it is almost forgotten that he was born at Stalnoye, Russia, in 1891 and that all through his childhood his family suffered the anti-Semitic persecution so much a part of Czarist Russia at that time.

He was the first of that astonishing procession of virtuosos to emanate from the St. Petersburg studio of the great violin teacher Leopold Auer, who taught Efrem Zimbalist, Jascha Heifetz, Nathan Milstein, Toscha Seidel, Michel Piastro and Eddy Brown.

Like so many artists, Elman endured poverty, misery, trial and struggle. Yet so great was his talent, and so beautiful the flow of sound he could evoke from the vibration of strings on a wooden box, that nothing could defeat him. Where Russian laws were against him, his music broke them down.

Elman was a prodigy who made his American debut in New York in 1908, at the age of seventeen, with the Russian Symphony Orchestra, playing the Tchaikovsky violin concerto. The concert was a success and Elman was accepted as a phenomenon.

But it was not until after the First World War, when he settled in New York, that he became a part of the American scene and a poster announcing an Elman concert affixed to the old yellow brick walls of Carnegie Hall meant a sell-out.

Howard Taubman, for years music editor of *The New York Times*, in writing of Elman emphasized the Elman tone, which he described as "warm, sensuous, opulent, as vibrant as a living thing . . . a hallmark of Elman's art, like the lights and shadows in Rembrandt."

JOHN ERSKINE

THIS is how he looked when I took his course at Columbia University, just before the onset of the Twenties. I sat in his classroom, hero-worshiping his quiet erudition, gentle humor, urbanity and sophistication. There were two great professors of English literature and the art of writing at Columbia University at that time. One was Brander Matthews, an iconoclastic firebrand whose lectures were showy; the other, John Erskine, whose course was a combination of the humanities, imagination and the common sense of writing. There was never a vacant chair when the latter taught, and nobody ever cut an Erskine class.

He was also a concert pianist, poet, scholar, administrator, composer, novelist, lecturer, librettist and Professor Emeritus of English, a great and well rounded man, artist and educator.

But what had a schoolteacher to do with the fireworks of the Twenties? In 1925 the staid and decorous college professor exploded into fame like one of the starbursts of a Fourth of July rocket and became a part of the history and tradition of those years with a book entitled *The Private Life of Helen of Troy*. This was a witty, salty and highly indecorous recounting in modern terms of the story of the adulterous elopement of the Greek housewife named Helen, which started the Trojan Wars.

The novel, followed by *Galahad*, his view of the somewhat priggish hero of *Le Morte d'Arthur*, was an immediate best-seller, topping the lists in the United States and Great Britain and becoming a byword. Dr. Erskine had won enduring fame.

Before his lamented passing at the age of seventy-two in 1951, he wrote opera librettoes, appeared as piano soloist with the New York Symphony Orchestra, became President of the Juilliard School of Music and wrote many other books. But it was upon the Twenties that he put the stamp of his personality when he took Helen of Troy out of the classical anthologies and made her a human being of flesh and blood.

DOUGLAS FAIRBANKS AND MARY PICKFORD

THE 1920's, more than any other time in our history, were ardent and fanciful; fairy-tale dreams of adolescent America turned into reality. A prize fighter made a million dollars in a night and married a society girl; the daughter of a German-American delicatessen proprietor swam the English Channel; a young, poor mail-plane pilot flew the Atlantic Ocean. Then there were the celebrated man and woman of the never-never land of the screen who fell in love and married in 1920, and this most sensational of screen true-life romances brought vicarious satisfaction to millions.

Douglas Fairbanks was the swashbuckling hero, envied and emulated by every red-blooded American boy, in such smash hits as *The Mark of Zorro, Robin Hood, The Three Musketeers, Don Q, The Black Pirate* and many others, while Mary Pickford, the actress known as "America's Sweetheart," was dominating the distaff side with *Tess of the Storm Country, Daddy Long-Legs, Pollyanna, Rebecca of Sunnybrook Farm, The Poor Little Rich Girl* and *Little Lord Fauntleroy.*

Both were inextricably bound up in the history of the rise of the motion picture from a five-cent peepshow to a billion-dollar industry. Their marriage was the culmination of the hero and heroine fantasies of a nation and one of the great sensations of ten years of sensations.

It was also the beginning of the end of innocence. Three years after the end of that glorious decade came the first rumors that the end of the romance was at hand, and there were reports that the disagreements had begun after their first and only co-starring venture, *The Taming of the Shrew.* There not only Kate and Petruchio clashed, but the temperaments and personal vanities of the two screen stars came into conflict. The dream was over and they were divorced in 1935. The Twenties had gone. Reality had arrived.

EDNA FERBER

THIS was the Edna Ferber of the mid-1920's, who received the Pulitzer Prize in 1925 for her novel *So Big*. She faced Muray's camera nervously and slightly defiantly for his *Vanity Fair* assignment, for the year before she had had a serious automobile accident. Yet, having made a fantastic recovery, she had finally consented to meet that supreme test, the all-seeing glass eye.

Thirty-five years later Muray photographed her again and the image is no different except that the curly auburn hair framing the strong, determined features is now white curly hair. Down through years after a decade that might reasonably have been considered the climax in a native American writer, she has continued to grow in stature.

During the sitting, Muray wrote, "we had fun. It was difficult to photograph her because she was chatting constantly." Her talk, he remembered, was the spilling over of a vital and fascinated woman who had more words inside her than could be set down on paper in the form of a series of fabulously successful novels and plays.

The stories for which she is best known, and which were created in that period, are timeless Americana, covering the United States of the past, such as *So Big*, *Show Boat* and *Cimarron*. These made some of the most stirring films ever to emerge from the Hollywood studios. With George Kaufman she wrote such plays as *The Royal Family*, *Dinner at Eight* and *Stage Door*. Her short stories were, and still are, considered classics of that vanishing art. For us who were young with her, she was one of our supreme storytellers. The Pulitzer committee crowned her as literary, but we who were reading her knew that whenever we saw her name on a magazine, the dust jacket of a novel or a theater marquee, there would be exciting entertainment.

F. SCOTT FITZGERALD

EVERY generation somehow manages to have its *minnesinger* to celebrate the emotions and protests of youth. As the Fifties had their Salinger, so did the Twenties see the rise of Francis Scott Key Fitzgerald, or Scott Fitzgerald for short: Irish-American, Princetonian, infantry lieutenant in World War I and usherer-in of the jazz age with his first novel, *This Side of Paradise*, published in 1920.

Fitzgerald not only wrote for the flaming youth, the young and disillusioned who were bidding farewell to the age of innocence, but he lived it for them as well. He was the first of a new kind of writer who produced his own image to become a legend while still alive. He married an unstable flapper. They drank. He spent the money that came pouring in, as it did upon all the newborn celebrities of the Twenties, in Paris, on the Riviera and in Rome.

Another like him was Ernest Hemingway, and Scott was *his* discoverer, for he wrote from Paris to Maxwell Perkins, his editor: "Dear Max: This is to tell you about a young man named Ernest Hemingway, who lives in Paris (an American), writes for the 'Transatlantic Review' and has a brilliant future. . . . I'd look him up right away. He's the real thing. . . . Scott."

But, for all his curious instability of character and his weaknesses, Fitzgerald was no flash-in-the-pan writer, as he proved by publishing his finest novel in 1925. *The Great Gatsby*, the story of the rise and fall of a bootlegger, was the perfect mirror held up to those spendthrift times when a bar became a social and necessary adjunct in the private home.

Fitzgerald, however, had one fatal flaw as a novelist. The unquestioned poet of the Twenties, he could strike the bell of his generation but of no other. That decade was but the blinking of an eyelid in the passage of time; was gone so quickly. Scottie could not adjust to the change.

ANTHONY FOKKER

OUR decade saw the beginning of the air age. In World War I, French, German, British and American knights of the air jousted in aircraft with chivalrous punctilio, but it was not until the Twenties that civilians began to get off the ground, and that largely due to the inventive genius and design of a Dutch-Javanese aviation engineer—Anthony Fokker. The first flight I ever made was in 1924 from London to Amsterdam, in a Fokker twelve-seater commercial monoplane.

Born in 1890 on the island of Java, where his father had a coffee plantation, Fokker was a failure at school, but as a young man of twenty he constructed his first monoplane in an abandoned zeppelin shed at Baden-Baden and taught himself to fly it. The Italian and British governments turned it down; the German Imperial Government did not, and the famous Fokker war plane with the Iron Cross painted on its side, firing its machine gun through the propeller, became a byword in World War I.

After the war Fokker, who never considered himself a German but rather a neutral inventor, fled to Holland and then came to the United States at the invitation of the U.S. Army Air Corps.

Only the real old-timers in aircraft production will remember Anthony Fokker's contributions to America's coming-of-age in the air during the 1920's. His three-engine plane (one on each wing and one at the nose), christened *Josephine Ford*, carried Richard E. Byrd and Floyd Bennett to the North Pole and became the prototype for the first American commercial transport planes. It was also the prototype for the first model airline operated between San Francisco and Los Angeles, and the base of today's American system of air transport.

JOHN GALSWORTHY

THE work of a great novelist throbs like a slow pulse through time, skipping generations for as long as thirty or forty years before the strong and inextinguishable beat is once more felt. John Galsworthy, graduate of Harrow and New College, Oxford, and quondam lawyer, was such a novelist, and the books comprising *The Forsyte Saga* are such a collective novel.

The five volumes, beginning with *The Man of Property* (1906), through *The Indian Summer of a Forsyte*, *In Chancery*, *Awakening* and *To Let*, tell the fictional history of upper-middle-class English society during the later Victorian and Edwardian eras. They were published at a time that enabled the new middle class not only to read and enjoy, but to see exactly the social chains from which, via World War I, it had escaped. Nickolas Muray was sent to photograph Galsworthy in his middle age, for the power of his books created a great curiosity among us to see what he looked like and to know more about him.

Like his contemporaries Arnold Bennett and H. G. Wells, Galsworthy was happiest living quietly in the country, out of the public eye. St. John Ervine once said of him, "He has written more than a dozen novels and at least a dozen plays but there is not one line in them to denote that he takes any interest whatsoever in John Galsworthy."

In 1893 Galsworthy, who had been admitted to the Bar, was fed up with law and went on a South Sea cruise aboard the sailing vessel *Torrens*. The First Mate of the ship was a Polish seaman by the name of Jozef Kordzeniowski, with whom he struck up a friendship. The officer showed him the manuscript of a novel he had written. It was called *Almayer's Folly*. The pen name on the first page was Joseph Conrad.

Galsworthy died in 1933. Thirty-odd years later he was rediscovered by a vast British public via television.

GRETA GARBO

TWO eyes, a nose and a mouth and their arrangement formed the magical personality of the most splendid creature of not only the Golden Decade but, so far, of the century as well.

There were great actresses, singers, dancers, sex symbols, It girls who trod the boards or flickered on celluloid during that grandiose era and momentarily held our attention or imagination, but Greta Garbo was our great romantic dream. No actress since has inspired such yearning, such vicarious participation in the glamorous exaltation of love and the worship of beauty. For she was incarnate that unattainable woman who haunts the dreams of every man and boy.

In 1920 Greta Louisa Gustafsson was a salesgirl in a department store in Stockholm, Sweden. Selected to appear in an advertising film, she won a scholarship to the Royal Dramatic Theater at the age of eighteen and was discovered by the Swedish director Moritz Stiller, who brought her to the attention of Louis B. Mayer in 1925. By 1928, when she had co-starred with John Gilbert in *Flesh and the Devil*, she had become the greatest box-office draw in the history of films.

When she and John Gilbert caught fire from each other and flamed into a real-life romance, every male and female participated. For it was more than sex and passion she portrayed: it was rather that distillation of Eros that is the despair of man.

Garbo is an actress as well as a perfect beauty, and a mystery too, and it was the mystery which added an extraordinary, unreal and dreamlike quality. For she would not give of herself to the public beyond what was seen upon the screen, and therefore she added to her attraction a thousand fancies and imaginings that haunted us. She alone would have made the decade memorable.

GEORGE GERSHWIN

W AS Gershwin the American Mozart? Like Mozart's, his melodic flame burned too brightly and he died too young. And as Mozart distilled the grace of his era into melody, so George Gershwin translated growing-up America into song and made the music by which we sang and danced our way through our decade. Like Mozart's, too, and unlike those of some contemporary American composers of light and even serious works, his compositions never stale. There is as much freshness and happiness in a Gershwin song today as when it was written.

The Brooklyn boy from Tin Pan Alley wrote the music for such remembered hits of our time as *Lady, Be Good, Oh, Kay!, Strike Up the Band, Funny Face, Girl Crazy* and the unforgettable *Of Thee I Sing*, as well as the melancholy harmonics of his Negro opera, *Porgy and Bess*.

Yet he meant most to us in the Twenties, those years of his fullest creative flowering, for he gave us our first sense of musical cultural security by confirming what our ears had hinted at already, that jazz was native American music and an original American contribution. Gershwin made its atonality and curious rhythms respectable with such concert-hall compositions as *Rhapsody in Blue, An American in Paris* and his piano concerto.

Gershwin's melodic line threads the twenties with veins of Gershwin sound, and he himself was one of the personalities, associated with the names of the day from Leopold Godowsky to Al Jolson, from Rubin Goldmark to Victor Moore. He accompanied Vivienne Segal, Eva Gauthier and Nora Bayes. He appeared in person as pianist under the baton of such conductors as Paul Whiteman, Walter Damrosch and Serge Koussevitzky. He gave weekly parties at which celebrities appeared; he came himself, smoking his big Havana cigar, to Muray's fencing soirees at his studio at the Park Central Hotel and held forth at the piano, playing and singing. He was young, gay, handsome, a genius and musically the spokesman and delight of our generation.

DOROTHY GISH

WHEN Dorothy Gish and her sister Lillian, older by two years, first worked as bit players for David Wark Griffith way back in 1912, he couldn't tell them apart and so he had Lillian wear a blue ribbon in her hair and Dorothy a red one. Then he would call out, "Blue Ribbon, enter here, crying," or, "Red Ribbon, you're on, laughing."

How instinctively right that he assigned to Lillian the delicate blue, the symbol of sadness, and to Dorothy the red ribbon of laughter. And this, in a sense, characterized the two sisters throughout their acting careers. Dorothy to some extent was always under the shadow of Lillian, and, strangely, it was Lillian who established Dorothy's comic potentialities. For it isn't generally known that in 1920 Lillian *directed* her younger sister in a comedy entitled *Remodeling a Husband*.

Griffith had to go to Florida, and Dorothy's contract with him called for one more picture. Lillian was convinced that no film in which they had ever played together had brought out Dorothy's sweetness and her sense of comic timing, and she undertook the project of directing this one. In Griffith's opinion the picture was the best that Dorothy ever made. The difference between the two sisters was once described by Lillian, who, speaking of her reserved manner, said, "When I go to a party, it stops being a party. On the other hand, Dorothy *is* the party."

Dorothy's most famous roles were in *Hearts of the World*, *Orphans of the Storm*, *The Bright Shawl*, *Romola*, *Nell Gwynn* and *Madame Pompadour*. In her first appearance, at the age of four in 1902, she played Little Willie in a road company touring with *East Lynne* at a salary of $15 a week, rescuing her family, which was broke at the time.

LILLIAN GISH

LILLIAN GISH was as delicate as a jasmine flower and her aura as exquisite. She was like a creation of Dante Gabriel Rossetti out of Botticelli, endowed with that innocence that pierced the heart of males of every age. The most hard-boiled critic of our times, George Jean Nathan, wrote of her, "The smile of the Gish girl is a bit of happiness trembling on a bed of death. The tears of the Gish girl . . . are the tears that Johann Strauss wrote in the Rosemary of his waltzes." And Joseph Hergesheimer compared her beauty to the "fragrant April moon of men's happiness." She was a symbol carried over from an era that still believed in feminine virtue and the special qualities of American womanhood.

A slender, virginal creature with finely chiseled features, she was loosed by D. W. Griffith into a make-believe world of villains bent upon doing her no good. She starred in the first great multi-reel films: *The Birth of a Nation, Intolerance, Broken Blossoms, Way Down East, Orphans of the Storm* and *The Scarlet Letter*.

On the screen she was harassed beyond endurance, but her face and form invaded our dreams, and her trials became our concern. Ten million knights stood ready to leap to horse and ride off in defense of her virtue.

She was more elf than girl; more child than woman. Tremulous, sensitive, dewy-eyed, as delicate and shy-appearing as a gazelle, she represented the romanticism of a nation that had not yet discovered shades of coloration either in fantasy or reality and saw life only in simple blacks and whites. There were only good guys and bad guys, chaste women and fallen sisters, and censors timed kisses with a stopwatch to make certain that no one in the audience boiled over.

She was an adolescent's dream, and no young man who saw her on the screen ever forgot her or thereafter could put her wholly out of mind. She was a soft, irresistible appeal to the protective instinct in the male.

ALMA GLUCK

AMERICA, just before, during and after World War I, was like a Roman candle spouting talents of every description. And one of these was the opera star and concert singer known as Alma Gluck, who, although not native-born American, came to this country when she was six and was a part of its musical renaissance.

She was born Reba Fiersohn in Bucharest, and after her parents emigrated in 1890, she grew up in New York, was educated in the public schools, Normal College and later Union College, to take a job as a stenographer and marry an employee of the Northwestern Mutual Life Insurance Company, Bernard Gluck.

Never once during all this time did the dark Rumanian beauty realize that she had a rich, clear and enthralling soprano voice. It was not until she was twenty-one, encouraged by her husband, that she began to think of singing professionally.

She made it all the way. Under the sponsorship of Geraldine Farrar, taught by Marcella Sembrich, she joined the famous Metropolitan Opera Company, sang Mimi in *La Bohème*, Nedda in *Pagliacci* and Marguerite in *Faust*. But the odd part of her resounding success story is that she was one of the first of the serious classical recording artists to make a fortune from the Victor Talking Machine Company, and, strangest of all, she made it with a recording which sold more than a million copies. It was "Carry Me Back to Old Virginny."

Divorced from Bernard Gluck, she became even more a part of the musical scene of that period when she married the violinist Efrem Zimbalist. Her concerts were sellouts. But in 1925 she retired from professional life and our famous Alma Gluck devoted herself to being Mrs. Zimbalist. Yet her talent lived and lives on through her daughter by her first marriage, the best-selling American novelist who writes under the name Marcia Davenport.

MARTHA GRAHAM

MARTHA GRAHAM, who went on to become America's greatest exponent of the dance, was a member of the Denishawn Company at the time she posed here for a page in *Vanity Fair.*

Of her Muray wrote: "She was innocent-looking and sweet; mobile like an Indian goddess, expressive not only with her fingers but with toes, chin, neck, the complete body. Her face and expressions were transformed into the spirit of the dance and she became supremely beautiful, although she was not off-stage considered a standard American beauty."

It is true she was not a beauty. Her face was long, gaunt, bony, but expressive of every emotion that flickered or flamed within her.

Whereas other dancers sought height with leaps and arabesques, Martha Graham went to earth, and her falls and use of the floor brought a new dimension to the art.

It was during the years 1927, 1928 and 1929 that she broke away to free herself forever from the surface theatrical devices of the dancing she had been doing, and even from her teachers, St. Denis and Shawn. Technically, it meant creating a system of movement that would free the body "to make visible the interior landscape," as she expressed it. Since that time she has never looked back.

Yet this rare mysterious Vestal of the dance was born to a physician in a suburb of Pittsburgh, grew up as an ordinary little girl who didn't even see a ballet until she was thirteen. Her family moved to Santa Barbara, California, where she attended private schools, and only then did she experience the urge to dance, despite her father's disapproval. And it was not until the year of his death, 1916, that she was able to enter the Denishawn School in Los Angeles.

LOUISE GROODY

HER nickname was Weezie. Her passion was standing clad in hip boots in an icy Pocono mountain stream, casting dry fly for trout. She was the first Broadway dancing star and musical-comedy actress to become a millionairess in those dollar days of the Twenties when a million was the money symbol and not just change out of a billion-dollar bill.

She entered this charmed circle because the brains of this tiny, blue-eyed, Texas-born girl were in her head as well as in her twinkling feet. She initiated the payment of a percentage of the show as well as a salary for her services. And when the musicals were such as *No, No, Nanette* and *Hit the Deck*, they piled up a fortune for her.

Not quite five feet tall, with chestnut hair and upswept nose, she posed for this camera study by Muray in 1925, and the hairdo tells a tale. For years Miss Groody's pride was her long curls, which, worn down her back, she made a part of her dancing as they swayed and swung to the rhythm of her feet. When Irene Castle made the Castle Bob popular, Louise Groody swore that she would never cut hers. But in 1925, on the opening night of *No, No, Nanette*, she caused a sensation by appearing with the most boyish bob of all. The show ran for two years, and *Hit the Deck* for two more. She never weighed more than a hundred pounds, but used to lose from two to three pounds each performance between rise and fall of the curtain.

Her second marriage ended in divorce and scandal when her husband, ex-stockbroker William McGee, was sentenced to Sing Sing for embezzling four million dollars. The millionaire dancing star was supposed to have been wiped out in the stock-market crash of 1929. But it wasn't true. One of the best-kept secrets of the era was that when her husband went to jail, Weezie sold out everything she had for something like a million and a half dollars to cover the losses of the small investors. She was greatly loved by all who knew her.

YVETTE GUILBERT

*E*NCYCLOPAEDIA BRITANNICA gives her birth date as 1868 with a question mark after it; at her death in 1944, *The New York Times* gave her age as seventy-nine. Somewhere in the long life of the great French *diseuse* Yvette Guilbert three years had been lost. When Nickolas Muray went to Paris in 1925 to photograph her, she was in her late fifties.

She was seen and heard in the United States only once, when, much against her will and seasick all the way, she came here on the S.S. *Olympia* in 1895. Interviewed in the old Savoy Hotel, she said, "Of course I'm glad to come to America. I wonder how the untraveled American will like me. I wonder if he will understand me. The lower classes in England didn't understand me a bit."

Why, then, did Frank Crowninshield feel that the Americans of the post-World War I decade would be interested in this French singer of naughty and macabre songs? It was because by then, although she had not reappeared here, the artist who had risen from the slums of Paris had achieved worldwide fame comparable to such contemporaries as Eleonora Duse, Sarah Bernhardt, the Goncourts, Zola, Daudet, Gounod, Edward VII, Monet, Renoir and, above all, Toulouse-Lautrec. For culture was breaking out all over, and if we had never heard the voice of Guilbert except on phonograph records, we were familiar with the famous poster that the stumpy little French artist had made of her: wide black hat, red hair, gaunt, ghastly, paper-white face, tight-fitting yellow dress and long black gloves.

In her day many an "untraveled" American didn't even know what *diseuse* meant and thought of Mlle. Guilbert as a singer. Her reaction was, "I even object to being called a songstress. I'm a *diseuse*—a reciter."

A British critic wrote of her in 1928: "If I were to characterise her genius, I would say she is the born painter of words. For the sounds that flow from her lips crystallise into canvas, design, colour and frame, visible to all who possess the faculty of perception."

WALTER HAMPDEN

WALTER HAMPDEN was *our* Shakespearean actor and in his day was acknowledged the best Hamlet since Edwin Booth.

His personality, his diction, his acting style were impeccably and impressively Stratford Shakespearean, but he was nevertheless our boy, born in 1879 in Brooklyn and educated at the Brooklyn Polytechnic Institute and Harvard University. In 1901, in his twenties, he went to England to understudy Sir Henry Irving and to acquire that English accent which led to the misconception that he was British. By the time the Twenties had been inaugurated, he was forty-one and at the full development of his powers.

Rivaling his cerebral, vocally exquisite and moving Hamlet was his interpretation of Rostand's tale of that large-nosed French duelist Cyrano de Bergerac, which so captured the imagination of audiences during the Twenties that he performed it more than a thousand times.

So popular was he that in 1925–1926 he leased the old Colonial Theatre on Broadway in the sixties, renamed it Hampden's Theatre and, with Ethel Barrymore co-starring, opened it in *Hamlet* and *The Merchant of Venice*. With these and other productions he filled the house nightly for almost two years.

He brought tremendous dignity to the American stage not only by his presence but by the plays he chose to offer audiences which were becoming more adult, such as *Caponsacchi*, Ibsen's *The Enemy of the People* and *Richelieu*.

The Village, that nursery of celebrities of the Twenties, counted him as one of its own, although he lived only on its fringe at 25 Fifth Avenue. But he often strolled the areas bordering Washington Square, dining in little Village restaurants, reserved, withdrawn, yet friendly and loved.

When in 1955 he died at the age of seventy-five, *The Villager*, the weekly newspaper of that colony, wrote: "Vale Walter Hampden! He was one of the galaxy of bright stars. In the Village his greatness was fully recognized, but here we knew him as a kindly neighbor, a courtly gentleman with old-school manners; here he found privacy."

HOPE HAMPTON

THERE was once a song entitled "Only a Bird in a Gilded Cage," and that was how the raucous press of the Twenties used to refer to a talented girl married to a millionaire, who was as much a part of the New York scene as the lights of Broadway, the Times Building in Times Square, bootleg liquor, the flapper and the Charleston.

This is Mrs. Jules Brulatour, known to us as the silent-motion-picture star Hope Hampton, and throughout the decade we lived with the story of her struggle to become an opera singer.

Hope had looks, voice, musicianship, even acting ability, but one oddly fatal handicap—too much money. The Brooklyn *Eagle* of 1928 told it this way:

"Fortunes have been spent to make girls into actresses and grand opera singers, but, with the exception of Ganna Walska, if the toll were taken, Hope Hampton perhaps would win the prize for having the most money expended on her grand opera career. Showmen were a little aghast the other day when it was announced that her husband, Jules Brulatour, is spending $5,000 for each rehearsal she has with the Philadelphia Grand Opera Company and to date he has poured something like a half a million dollars into her career."

Brulatour, who married her in 1923, made his millions through acquiring interest in patents which brought him royalties for every foot of motion-picture film used in the United States.

This was the kind of *True Confessions* real-life drama that we loved—"Millionaire Tries to Make Opera Singer of Movie Queen."

Although she sang successfully with the Philadelphia Grand Opera, the Paris Opéra-Comique and the Chicago Grand Opera and was given the *Légion d'Honneur* while singing in Paris, she never truly made it in the U.S. as a singer. Critics were suspicious of her because she had bought her way into grand opera; operatic managers saw her husband simply as a goldmine to be exploited.

But how she decorated our scene.

JEAN HARLOW

JEAN HARLOW was the success story with the unhappy ending: the "extra girl" who first popularized platinum-colored hair and, characterized as the Blonde Bombshell, died in Hollywood in 1937 at the age of twenty-six, at the height of her career in films.

She was perhaps the first to nourish the great American breast fetishism which dared to come out into the open in that decade. Of course, no one went to the lengths of today's exposure, and the word used was "cleavage." And if too much of the space between the two breasts was shown, censors drew long faces and ordered cuts.

Muray went to a studio wingding in Hollywood, thrown at the time he went out to photograph Jean Harlow, who was then filming *Dinner at Eight*. The party was a reception for a producer, Peter Freuchen. Muray noted, "Freuchen was introduced to Jean and simply could not take his eyes off the low gown which almost exposed her beautiful bosom. When she shook hands with him he didn't look up, but asked, 'Are they real?' Jean merely laughed, 'Look—no straps.' "

She exploded like a firework in the late Twenties, when, from a girl hanging about Hollywood's Central Casting Bureau, she emerged as the leading lady of Howard Hughes' *Hell's Angels*. She flamed across the American screen as a gay, voluptuous gold-digger type, stoking the libidos of American husbands married to fat, dowdy, sexless wives. She was a talented woman, but scandal dogged her and she was among those who set the pattern for the kind of tragic end typified in recent times by Marilyn Monroe.

Tributes by her co-workers were characteristic when she died. W. S. Van Dyck, who directed her, said: "She leaves us at the height of a glorious career; a great actress and an even greater friend." And the ghost writer for Louis B. Mayer: "This is the end of a rich personal friendship. This girl whom so many millions adored was one of the loveliest, sweetest persons I have known in thirty years of the theatrical business. I have lost a friend—the world has lost a ray of sunlight."

JED HARRIS

HE was one of the boy wonders of the decade. Born to Meyer and Esther Horowitz, Jed Harris was just twenty and a Yale graduate in 1920; by 1929 he had produced some of the most sensational theatrical hits of the period.

He served his apprenticeship in show business, first as a New York reporter, then a writer for the theatrical magazine *Billboard*, edging always closer to the theater as a tub thumper and finally advance agent for shows trouping the country.

Five years of this schooling and he was ready. In 1925 he produced his first show, called *Weak Sisters*, and simultaneously got his first flop out of his system. It didn't even check the career of a boy who only a few years before, when he was broke and jobless, had slept on a Bryant Park bench in lieu of a bed. He came back with another play in 1926 called *Love 'Em and Leave 'Em* and broke even. And then in the fall of that same year, on September 16, he unveiled the sensational melo-drama *Broadway*, known as the million-dollar success, and Jed Harris was made.

He was then twenty-six years old and the uncrowned King of Broadway. Between that time and the end of the decade he produced *Spread Eagle*, *Coquette*, *The Royal Family*, *The Front Page* and *Serena Blandish*.

In addition he managed to be inextricably enmeshed with the rise and happiness of three of the other personages in this volume: George Abbott, who worked with him on both *Love 'Em and Leave 'Em* and *Broadway;* Helen Hayes, who starred in *Coquette;* and Charles MacArthur, who married her after the smash hit made by *The Front Page*, which he wrote with Ben Hecht.

HELEN HAYES

THERE probably has never been a Cleopatra like this mischievous minx before or after, but this is how Helen Hayes saw the character when she played it in the Theatre Guild's production of *Caesar and Cleopatra* in 1925.

On the back of one of the proofs of this sitting is scribbled, "Both Helen and I liked this for a change of pace." Muray noted: "These pictures still induce shock in viewers who couldn't dissociate her from Victoria Regina." For, of course, the part of the young-to-old English Queen was the most notable of Helen Hayes' many roles.

But she was already a famous actress, having trod the boards at the age of five as Prince Charles in *The Royal Family* and subsequently as Little Lord Fauntleroy and in the dual part in *The Prince and the Pauper*.

She was celebrated, too, as the wife of that half-faun Charles MacArthur, newspaperman and playwright. And what old-timers who see the decade in a rosy glow will remember is an arbitration board's decision that the daughter resulting from this union was an act not of man, but of God—and that the child was therefore known as "The Act of God Baby." For in 1929, while Miss Hayes was starring in *Coquette* on tour, she had to withdraw from the cast and the play closed. The producer, Jed Harris, pointed to a contract clause stipulating, "The Management is not responsible for fire, strike, or act of God." Six actors, however, held out for a week's wages coming to them under their Equity contracts, maintaining that Jehovah was not involved. God and Jed Harris won.

JASCHA HEIFETZ

YOUNG Heifetz, here portrayed early in the Twenties, was an infant wonder. For, born at Vilna, Russia, in 1901, he began the study of the violin at the age of three, entered the Royal School of Music at Vilna at five and was graduated four years later.

When he came to the U.S. for his New York debut in 1917, he was already a veteran of the concert hall. He gave his first recital in St. Petersburg at the advanced age of ten.

In 1925 he became an American citizen and a part of the glowing musical tapestry of the decade.

Muray and Heifetz became fast friends, and when the time came for a more mature photograph, Muray was summoned.

The sitting was scheduled for two o'clock. Nick, the psychologist, set the stage, borrowing a record player together with one of Jascha's latest albums from The Gramophone Shop downstairs, and then sat biting his fingernails as no Heifetz turned up.

An hour later, rather furtively, in came Jascha carrying two violin cases and a large, paper-wrapped package. He had got lost at the gadget counter of a famous hardware store.

Wasting no words, since he had a second appointment at four o'clock, Muray asked, "Where the hell have you been?" and told his assistant to start the record player. No more than two or three bars could have come forth before Heifetz jumped from the stool, crying, "Stop playing that!" He explained that he could not possibly relax while listening to his "mistakes." Muray sent someone down to The Gramophone Shop to get an album of someone else's mistakes. From then on there was no hitch. The shots took full advantage of his delicate expressions, and of his strong, sensitive, beautiful hands poised on bow and strings.

JOHN HELD, JR.

THE years have rolled over and obliterated the answer to the question as to which came first, the flapper of the Twenties, the Sheba with her coonskin-coated, hip-flask-toting Sheik, or the drawings of her by the late John Held, Jr., the Leonardo of Flaming Youth. His subjects were the shingled girls with rolled stockings wearing the ancestor of the mini-skirt, their knees as well as their lips rouged, flat-chested and swivel-hipped, and their boy-friends who affected bell-bottomed trousers, parted their hair in the middle and slicked it down, and played ukeleles.

We saw them by the thousands in the Yale Bowl on football Saturdays, or swinging their legs in the Black Bottom and Charleston in cafés and speakeasies. Held was the man who immortalized them and fixed them forever with his drawings of the youth of the red-hot jazz age: Joe College and Betty Coed strutting their stuff at fraternity hops and spiked-tea parties, or necking in the rumble seat of a Stutz Bearcat.

Yet, oddly, the creative genius who caught an era with his pen was some fifteen years older than the crazy kids he depicted, never went to college, hated crowds and could not be dragged to a cocktail party. Further, he was a Mormon.

He was born in Salt Lake City in 1889, with an art teacher for a father and an accomplished actress for a mother. His life impinged upon those of two other men who were great celebrities. A schoolmate and colleague on a student newspaper was Harold Ross, who was later to found *The New Yorker*, and in later life Held drew the illustrations for F. Scott Fitzgerald's *Tales of the Jazz Age*.

Like all the ambitious youth of the day, he gravitated to New York, where he arrived in 1910 with exactly $4 in his pocket. It was in 1922 that the first of the flappers, who came to be known as "Held's Angels," appeared on the cover of *Judge* and he was away—an overnight sensation. William Randolph Hearst paid him $2,500 a week for a daily flapper cartoon strip entitled "Oh, Margy."

JOSEPH HERGESHEIMER

JOSEPH HERGESHEIMER wrote his finest novels between 1914 and 1933, turning out a book a year during that period, some of them historical and others holding up the mirror to the more blatant foibles of his times.

When I was a young man taking writing courses, we read Hergesheimer not only for the authenticity of his writing, his precise, distinguished and compact style, but also for his shining example of perseverance and refusal to be discouraged. For it was pointed out to us that he had written steadily for something like twelve to fourteen years without selling so much as a line.

During his era he achieved what few American writers could duplicate—publication and serialization in *The Saturday Evening Post*, to which every young writer of my times aspired as the first goal, as well as having his novels accepted as a serious contribution to American literature.

The Saturday Evening Post, which probably achieved its highest circulation figures during the Twenties, was read by millions, but was denigrated as a "slick" magazine: slick in the coated stock on which it was printed and slick in the type of stories it published, aimed at entertaining the family. Once a popular writer was tarred with *Post* money, he could search in vain for literary laurels.

But not Joe Hergesheimer. Born a Quaker in 1880, he produced such classic tales as *The Three Black Pennies, Java Head, The Bright Shawl, Tampico, Swords and Roses* and, like other novelists of his day, provided material for the movies, which then were as insatiable for stories as television is today. Dorothy Gish lists *The Bright Shawl* among her most important pictures, and Leatrice Joy was a success in *Java Head*.

HELEN HOKINSON

ONE wonders whom and what Helen Hokinson would have drawn if she had been born thirty or so years earlier. The shy girl with the whimsical mouth, large eyes and tousled hair was one of America's most amusing artist-humorists, and her subject was the middle-aged wives of the United States and their activities in suburban clubs, gardens, flower shows, charity bazaars and kindred affairs. She caricatured the country's women of leisure at their self-appointed labors acquiring culture, or just passing time.

But before the advent of the twentieth century there was practically no such thing as leisure for women. Good works were confined to the wealthy. There was then no vast suburban middle class sufficiently affluent to be able to give the time to hear lectures on current authors, band together for community improvement or attend parent-teacher meetings.

But they were there in the Twenties, apparently sprung full-panoplied, their pouter-pigeon bosoms draped in shapeless frocks, Queen Mary hats upon their heads, archly occupying rostrums, handing out prizes at pet or flower shows, "trying on" in the matrons' department of Fifth Avenue stores. They gathered for afternoon bridge, tea and cake parties in their suburban, pseudo-Tudor homes. And Helen Hokinson was drawing them for *The New Yorker*—some 1,698 hilarious cartoons in her lifetime.

She was born in Mendota, Illinois, shortly before the 1900's—it was her little joke that she refused to reveal her age—and studied at the Academy of Fine Arts in Chicago, specializing in fashion drawing. Her arrival in New York in 1921 was unheralded. Bored with fashion drawing, she began to look at the women all around her. Her overwhelming sense of humor did the rest.

Her death in 1949 was a tragedy and an irony. For she was on her way to a luncheon in Washington, where she was to address wives of the Justices of the Supreme Court, wives of Cabinet Secretaries, wives . . . Her plane crashed.

LOUISE HOMER

SHE was born Louise Dilworth Beatty, the daughter of a Presbyterian minister in Pittsburgh. In the period 1923–1924 the National Association of Women Voters selected her as one of the twelve greatest living American women. Her mother, who numbered some twenty ministers in her family, had never been in a theater or a place of amusement of any kind until she heard Louise Homer sing in *Faust* and *Aïda* with the Metropolitan Opera Company in Philadelphia.

Louise, when a student in Boston, married Sidney Homer, her harmony teacher. She became an opera singer after her husband took her to Paris to have her fine contralto voice trained.

Her career abroad was a switch on the usual operatic story of the foreigner invading America. Mme. Homer made her debut at Vichy, sang at Covent Garden and the Royal Théâtre de la Monnaie in Brussels, and was commanded to appear at Buckingham Palace before the Prince and Princess of Wales.

For nineteen years, from 1900 on, she was the contralto mainstay of the old Metropolitan Opera House, singing with such stars as Caruso, Scotti, Gadski, Alma Gluck and Geraldine Farrar. She sang Amneris in the most notable *Aïda* ever performed, with Emmy Destinn as Aïda, Caruso as Radames and, in the pit, Arturo Toscanini making his New York bow. Again with Toscanini conducting, she set the town on fire with Gadski and Alma Gluck, singing Orfeo in *Orfeo ed Euridice*.

But, above all, she was a kind, gentle, wonderful woman, the most admired and best beloved of American-born singers, and the mother of six children. When she died in 1947, Dr. Hamilton Holt, President of Rollins College, where in her later years she taught music, said: "Louise Homer was a blessing to her home, her country and her art. She had both quality and simplicity. She walked with kings but never lost the common touch. She had a tender heart and an upright mind."

MR. AND MRS. HERBERT HOOVER

HERE are Herbert and Lou Hoover, the thirty-first President of the United States and his First Lady. For years this man, who in two world wars functioned as the greatest administrator of relief and organizer of food shipments to starving countries, unjustly suffered the stigma of having been the cause of the great crash and depression of 1929.

Today we know that he merely had the bad luck to be in office at the time, succeeding Calvin Coolidge, who, with Yankee shrewdness, had chosen not to run.

The depression was caused by a concatenation of circumstances that no one human being could have stopped: a combination of uncontrolled greed for easy money, the orgy of stock speculation in the late Twenties, the policy of the Federal Reserve Board's inflation of credit, and the unhampered shenanigans of European financiers.

The late Herbert Hoover's term in the White House, until he suffered a humiliating defeat at the hands of Franklin D. Roosevelt, was a misery of near-panic, bread lines, "bonus marchers" and non-stop criticism by the nation's press. He was made a whipping boy for the calamities and unrelieved sin of the spree upon which we launched at the beginning of the decade without once pausing to consider the consequences.

Yet history today looks upon the late President Hoover as one of our greatest Americans and a man who, long before the crash came, gave warning as a private individual that it must come. When he took office, it was too late to stem the disaster.

The man in the high collar facing Muray's camera was shaken by the avalanche of bitterness and criticism, but never defeated. Called upon once more to take on the work of relief after World War II, he duplicated and surpassed his feats performed in World War I and through his eighty-first year continued in government service as an unparalleled organizer.

HEDDA HOPPER

MISS ELDA FURRY, born in 1890 in Hollidaysburg, Pennsylvania, of Quaker parents, endured a staid and stifled childhood which was not alleviated until she was seventeen, when Ethel Barrymore, on tour in *Captain Jinks of the Horse Marines*, passed through nearby Altoona and Elda sneaked off into the balcony. A year later Miss Furry ran away to New York to become an actress.

She got a job in the chorus of an opera company and made her way dancing, singing and doing bit parts around New York theaters, until she met one of the most renowned actors of the day, De Wolf Hopper. He made her his fifth wife.

Mr. Hopper's previous wives had been named Ella, Nella, Ida and Edna. Elda was just one too much, and after consulting a numerologist, Elda Hopper became Hedda Hopper and a national character was born. Although she divorced Mr. Hopper in 1922, she never changed the name that she was later to make famous as one of the two most powerful Hollywood gossip columnists.

The Twenties knew her as a not particularly outstanding actress who appeared in such pictures as *Virtuous Wives*, *Sherlock Holmes*, *Don Juan* and *Mona Lisa*. Yet we were conscious of the presence of Hedda Hopper as part of the Broadway and Hollywood scene. It would not have been possible to ignore such a flamboyant personality. This was how she looked in the Twenties, before the late Alicia Patterson—daughter of Joe Patterson, publisher of the *Daily News*—discovered that Hedda sucked in gossip as a vacuum cleaner sucks in dirt, and could return it tinctured with acid. She gave herself an image by indulging in outrageous hats that became a kind of trademark. She was the successful rival of the one and only "Lolly," Louella Parsons, and a holy terror until, rich and feared, she died at the age of seventy-five in 1966.

VLADIMIR HOROWITZ

TODAY'S generation knows Vladimir Horowitz as "the man who came back," the concert pianist who, after retiring from public performance for twelve years, returned a different person and a different artist, to stun an adoring public less with his virtuosity than with his deep sensitivity and musicianship.

The reason for his retirement was that somehow the Russian boy from Kiev, twenty-four years old when he sat for Muray, had got off on the wrong foot. He was too much of a pianistic acrobat and juggler. Of all the instruments, the piano seemed to whip American music-lovers into the greatest pitch of adulation, as witness the early receptions given to such as Paderewski.

Horowitz at the time of his American debut in the late Twenties was no less lionized. His introduction to our country was featured by an on-stage duel between himself and the British conductor Sir Thomas Beecham, who was likewise making his American bow in 1928. Beecham, who was conducting without a score, either had forgotten the tempo of the Tchaikovsky concerto or deliberately wanted to play it slowly. Horowitz had other ideas. For the first two movements Vladimir followed the baton. For the last he took off by himself, leaving Beecham helplessly trying to catch up as best he could. At the finish the audience hysterically screamed its approval of the new pianist, and Olin Downes, music critic of *The New York Times*, wrote: "Blood is blood. The cry of the wild is heard whether it is a savage beating a drum or a young Russian mad with excitement, physical speed and power pounding on a keyboard." Someone said he seemed to have a third hand.

When, some twenty-two years later, disgust with his performances and fatigue had overtaken Horowitz, he retired, never touched a keyboard for a year, and for the next eleven relearned playing the piano with tenderness and love instead of muscle, bone and sinew.

LANGSTON HUGHES

IN 1947, when the American Negro poet, novelist and dramatist Langston Hughes was forty-five, he spent seven cold, dismal hours at Atlanta airport when bad weather grounded his plane, for no taxicab would take a Negro back to town. He could not even get a cup of hot coffee at the luncheon counter, for no one would sell him one. The author of *Not Without Laughter*, *The Weary Blues*, *Shakespeare in Harlem* and a dozen novels must have thought of a poem he wrote in which a child speaks, asking:

> Where is the Jim Crow section
> On this merry-go-round, Mister,
> Cause I want to ride . . . ?

But in the Twenties this handsome boy was "discovered" during a curious Negro renaissance when black poets, novelists, singers, dancers and actors were "taken up" by liberals and literary white folk.

For the Negro it must have been the most humiliating time of all, because he was being patronized by a society that was preening itself, saying, "Look how broad-minded we are!"

It was the time of the Cotton Club in Harlem, and it was the custom for jaded café society and speakeasy hoppers to finish off the night with a trip up to Harlem to see the all-Negro show and watch the dancers. There were a few sincere admirers of flowering Negro talent such as Carl Van Vechten and Vachel Lindsay, Kurt Weill and Elmer Rice, with whom Langston Hughes wrote the Broadway musical *Street Scene*, but for the most part the interest of the whites in the coloreds in those days was as false as a $3 bill.

But there was nothing phony about the late Langston Hughes or his distinguished ancestry—a grandfather died fighting with John Brown at Harpers Ferry; a grand-uncle was a Virginia Congressman and a U.S. Minister to Haiti. Hughes struggled his way through college and earned his first money with poems that were published in *Vanity Fair* and *The New Republic* in 1923.

FANNIE HURST

THE Twenties were notable for producing women who were not only famous novelists, but eccentric and startling characters as well. They came mostly out of the Midwest to the Mecca of New York, there to create literature and legend.

Fannie Hurst's birthplace was Hamilton, Ohio; her ancestry, Bavarian; her parents' home, St. Louis, Missouri. She was educated at Washington University in St. Louis. Her parents were prosperous; there was no need for her to write, beyond the compulsion of internal fire. During her senior year at college she sent thirty-five of her stories to *The Saturday Evening Post* and received thirty-five rejection slips. Years after her graduation they accepted the thirty-sixth.

In 1910 Miss Hurst was swallowed up by New York, where she divided her time between social research and the vain battering at doors of editorial offices. Her persistence in the face of a long and consistent period of disappointments, frustrations and worse was extraordinary.

Then, without warning, success came and practically overnight the lonely, gawky girl from the Midwest found the magazines clamoring for her short stories. The Twenties saw her flower from a nationally known short-story writer to an internationally recognized novelist. Of these, her best known, *Star-dust*, appeared in 1921, *Lummox* in 1923, *Appassionata* in 1926, *A President is Born* in 1928, *Five and Ten* in 1929 and *Back Street* in 1931—all of them translated into fourteen languages.

She acquired a husband and a trademark: the husband, Jacques S. Danielson, pianist and composer; the trademark, the calla lily, with which her home was always filled.

Her marriage to Danielson was revealed only after five years, when she startled newspaper readers by announcing that she and her husband maintained separate apartments and met for breakfast twice a week.

MICHIO ITO

THE American life following World War I threw up all sorts of oddball characters, artists and geniuses, and one who decorated the theatrical scene and whose name was on the lips of the dance devotees was a Japanese by the name of Michio Ito. I used to meet him during my Village days at those innocently pagan rites known as The Greenwich Village Ball.

He was born in 1893 in Kyoto, into a family of seven children, all boys and all of them theatrically talented. We first saw and heard of Ito when he appeared in 1920–1921 in John Murray Anderson's production of *The Greenwich Village Follies*, the same show that introduced Margaret Severn dancing in her Benda masks.

The paths of Michio and Muray crossed. In his column for *Dance* Magazine of February 1928, called "Nickolas Muray Looks at the Dance," Nick wrote:

"The most unusual concert in ideas and presentation was given at the John Golden Theater by Michio Ito—a finished performance that one seldom encounters. Four different groups, each one a gem and perfectly executed in every detail, gave the audience a continued thrill."

From his review of the evening develops the curious fact that Ito combined Oriental movement and interpretation with Western music. In the "Bu Yoh" of a group of Chinese numbers in a white costume and headdress, with ivory-toned screens for background, he danced to the music of Ravel. A Japanese spear dance was performed to Tchaikovsky, and he seems to have brought the evening to a close with the "Golliwog's Cakewalk" by Debussy.

Later, Ito headed a dancing school in Hollywood and an operatic and choreographic school in San Francisco. He returned to Japan after the Second World War and died in Tokyo in 1961.

AL JOLSON

THE songs and the voices one remembers best are those of one's youth: Al Jolson pleading with his "Mammy," "Sonny Boy," "April Showers" and "Avalon," and the rich, curious style of the onetime minstrel man.

Today's generation will never so much as have heard of Lew Dockstader, and the old Minstrel Show is as much a thing of the past as *The Drunkard* or Barnum's Museum. But Dockstader's Minstrels toured the nation at the century's turn, with Mr. Interlocutor in burnt cork quizzing Mr. Bones and the End Men bursting into solos, and this was all the theater that many American hamlets ever saw.

In this kind of rough trouping, young Asa Yoelson, born in Washington, D.C., in 1886 to a Jewish cantor, got his training. J. J. Shubert heard him sing with the Minstrels and hired him for the famous Winter Garden shows—musical revues which rivaled Ziegfeld's *Follies* and George White's *Scandals*. Jolson's voice, his gestures and his dynamism became part of the Broadway scene, and by the time the great decade began, he was recognized as America's greatest single entertainer.

It was Al Jolson who, after having failed in silent movies, was credited with revolutionizing motion pictures when in 1927 the first breakthrough was achieved with the sound films. It was the Warner Brothers who gambled, producing *The Jazz Singer*, with Jolson caroling away in a story not unlike his own adventurous life. The film was an instantaneous success, grossed five million dollars and revitalized Hollywood. The following year he made *The Singing Fool*, in which he first gave forth with "Sonny Boy," resulting in a sale of more than a million records.

He died in 1950 at the age of sixty-four, from a heart attack brought on by the strenuous entertaining of troops from Alaska to the Southwest Pacific, from England to North Africa, India and Brazil, and a fatal final tour of duty with the USO in Korea.

ROBERT TYRE JONES, JR.

M Y friend Jones would be the first to deny that he was this beautiful, and I doubt further that he would have been wearing a ring on his finger while swinging a club. But here are the straight left arm, the cocked wrists and the concentration characteristic of Bobby Jones, wizard, shaman and high priest of the national mystery known as golf.

Jones meant something special to us in those days. Around the turn of the century, golf was practically a private game; courses were few and its addicts had to be wealthy. In 1913 a twenty-year-old American amateur, a former caddy, Francis Ouimet of Boston, first tied and then beat the great English professional stars Harry Vardon and Ted Ray in the Open Championship. Suddenly everybody wanted to play. But it was not until the close of World War I that Americans found the money and the leisure to indulge, and by the end of the decade 1920–1930 golf courses in the country had multiplied to more than 5,000, and there were some 5,000,000 addicts and worshippers at the shrine of Jones.

For Jones, too, was an amateur and still today he ranks as the finest golfer the country has ever produced. And furthermore, he was an amateur who regularly beat the professionals and climaxed ten years of sensational tournament victories on both sides of the Atlantic by his incredible Grand Slam in 1930, when he won the British Open, the British Amateur, the American National Open and the American National Amateur championships. The odds against him were astronomical.

Of the five million golfers, 4,990,000 were duffers hacking, sclaffing, topping, slicing, shanking their way around the country's courses on weekends, throwing clubs, cursing, moaning, shedding tears of frustration as the art of the game of self-discipline eluded them.

For us who belonged to this fraternity, there was always Jones, who, too, once had thrown clubs and wept at his own failures and now had it made—the exquisitely perfect golfing machine, sportsman and one of the best-loved sports figures of the era.

HELEN KELLER

OF all the photographs taken by Nick Muray of the celebrities of his day, the one capturing the delicate wisp of a smile on the face of this lovely girl is perhaps the most moving. For it is of one whose eyes are sightless and ears unhearing.

Helen Keller is eighty-seven today, and if this generation remembers her or knows who she is, it is by virtue of a play about her called *The Miracle Worker*, exquisitely acted by child actress Patty Duke with Anne Bancroft in the role of Miss Anne Sullivan, the teacher. It was the real Anne Sullivan who accomplished the miracle of penetrating the darkness in which Helen Keller lived and bringing her substitutes for sight and hearing, enabling her to become one of the most admired women of our times.

When Miss Sullivan came to the child, Helen was a little girl living in a vacuum, shut off from all contact with the world and with no concept of anything beyond eating and eliminating. But she had a spark and a great courage, and Miss Sullivan found them. In three years, by hand signals, she had taught Helen the alphabet and also to read and to write. In 1904, after four years at Radcliffe, always with Anne Sullivan at her side to telegraph the sense of the lectures to her, Miss Keller graduated *cum laude*.

The Mona Lisa smile captured by Muray is that of a woman who has overcome every obstacle, every handicap and at no time during her long and useful life has yielded to self-pity or let herself be patronized. Her life's work was with the American Foundation for the Blind.

Anne Sullivan died in 1936, in many ways as remarkable a woman as Helen Keller.

MADGE KENNEDY

IN my adolescent years I was in love vicariously with a number of stage and screen actresses, notably Lillian Gish, Mae Marsh, Marilyn Miller, but mostly Miss Madge Kennedy, to whom, as I remember, I remained faithful longer than to most. For there was something particularly appealing in this whimsical ingenue comedienne who had the gift of turning farces such as *Twin Beds* and *Fair and Warmer*, in which she starred, into the cleanest, most delightful and somehow most innocent-seeming comedies. She could cavort about the stage in a nightie for an evening, practically without arousing so much as a single lascivious thought in the minds of clean-living upholders of American womanhood.

True, the garments were then of solid, non-transparent cotton, and a few years ago Miss Kennedy—today still vibrant and vital at seventy years of age—expressed considerable shock at the frothy gauze of the movie non-nighties of the present.

Then she had that quality which could start a vogue, and in the Twenties there was a definite Madge Kennedy cult. Girls had a difficult time making up their minds whether they wanted to be cuddlesome like Madge or supercharged and steamy like Theda Bara or Nita Naldi.

Yet she wasn't actually a type, but a highly competent actress, as indicated by her performance in a heavily dramatic and emotional dual role in the drama *Cornered*, which opened in 1920.

Her versatility was characteristic of our times. In 1923, melodrama left behind, she was adorable with the incomparable comedian W. C. Fields in *Poppy*, and thence to yet another kind of role in Philip Barry's *Paris Bound*.

She was, and still is, a refreshing person, for in summing up her career—which began at art school, whence she gravitated to the stage—she writes: "This is no saga of difficult, stern, barren years. Everything just seemed to unfold and I only had to be there, ready to give whatever I had to give."

I still love her.

EVELYN LAW, MARY LEWIS, MARTHA LORBER, MARY EATON

READING from left to right, this high-powered quartet from the *Ziegfeld Follies of 1922*, the sixteenth annual production of this extravaganza, consists of Evelyn Law, Martha Lorber, Mary Lewis and Mary Eaton. This was how the great Florenz Ziegfeld liked his female stars to look. And since he liked it, so did we: the figures ample and the costumes practically indescribable.

In the *New York Times* review of the opening night of this show, the Misses Law and Eaton are given credit for doing most of the dancing, with the latter also being credited for vocalizing. But the great voice of the show belonged to the statuesque Mary Lewis, acknowledged as the prima donna.

All four of these dolls were famous personalities of the Twenties. Martha Lorber came to the *Ziegfeld Follies* via the Russian ballet master Fokine and Michio Ito. And Mary Lewis was one of two opera stars who graduated from the *Ziegfeld Follies* to the Metropolitan Opera House, where she became one of the great-name performers in such roles as Marguerite in *Faust*. Her career started in a church choir. In 1918 she was still singing and playing the violin and organ in churches in Dallas and Little Rock. In 1919 she ran away from home and in 1920 got a job in the *Greenwich Village Follies* and was promoted to prima donna before the show opened. Thence to Ziggy.

Mary Eaton and Evelyn Law battled their way up from child actresses, and the former is perhaps best remembered for her starring role with the perpetual-motion comedian Eddie Cantor in *Kid Boots*.

The prodigal Ziegfeld, one of the greatest showmen of the era, whose slogan was that the *Follies* glorified the American girl, collected them all under one roof for the price of one ticket, along with such further attractions as Will Rogers, Gallagher and Shean, Gilda Gray and, for good measure, the Tiller Girls.

It was in this show that Will Rogers, twirling his lariat, quipped, "If it doesn't glorify the American girl, it certainly exposes her."

D. H. LAWRENCE

HOW curious in these days of the emancipation of the four-letter word to look back upon David Herbert Lawrence, his times and struggles with the censors. Escape from the Victorian strait-jacket was not accomplished without backlash from the bluenoses. James Branch Cabell's *Jurgen*, with never a dirty word from cover to cover, was banned in Boston, and Lawrence's novels attracted the attention of the British Home Office, John S. Sumner, Secretary of the Society for the Suppression of Vice, as well as the police of Boston and Philadelphia. Lawrence's last novel, *Lady Chatterley's Lover*, had to be printed privately in Europe in 1928 and only a few years ago achieved the freedom of general sale throughout the United States without fear of the gendarmes.

However, this son of a Nottingham coal miner was one of the first great truly modern novelists, whose early books, *The White Peacock*, *The Trespasser* and *Sons and Lovers*, the latter adjudged possibly his best, were being read in America by intellectuals when they could lay their hands on them. And in the Twenties, with poems and further novels, *Women in Love*, *The Plumed Serpent*, *Aaron's Rod* and *Kangaroo*, he became a "name."

Muray notes: "I photographed D. H. Lawrence in my MacDougal Street studio in 1920. He was sent to me by Frank Crowninshield for *Vanity Fair*, and was brought down to the studio, bodily, by Mabel Dodge, the heiress and well-known, if eccentric, patroness of the arts.

"Had you met D. H. Lawrence on the street, you would never have thought him a great writer or thinker. His long beard and mustache were unkempt; his hair was disheveled, as was his attire. The shirt he wore was three sizes larger than he needed, and he looked as if he had borrowed it from a poor uncle. Nor have I ever seen a person more shy. I finally managed to quell Mrs. Dodge's flow of words and began to talk to Lawrence about his work. Once his attention was engaged, I had no difficulty in exposing about a dozen very good negatives. There wasn't a single smiling picture, but he wasn't the smiling type."

GERTRUDE LAWRENCE

WHEN at the age of fifty-two unexpected death came for Gertrude Lawrence, one of the golden creatures of a golden era was taken from us.

The year was 1952 and she was then playing Anna Leonowens in the Rodgers-and-Hammerstein musical play *The King and I*. But she belonged to us of the Twenties when in 1924 she first came to New York with *Charlot's Revue*, appearing with Beatrice Lillie and Jack Buchanan and singing a number called "Limehouse Blues."

The melody remains embedded along with the strange, throaty voice of Gertrude Lawrence. I have never forgotten the electric glow of her personality. From that night on, New York was at her feet.

It is odd how often the lives of the people who eventually became sitters to the Muray camera intermingled or impinged upon one another. When Gertrude Lawrence was nine, she was studying acting in London with Italia Conti. Another of the students at that same studio was a boy by the name of Noel Coward. A year later she was one of fifty girls playing in the chorus of Max Reinhardt's production of *The Miracle*, which called for a hundred child choristers; Coward was one of the fifty boys. Later he was to write two of her greatest successes: *Private Lives* and *Tonight at 8:30*. George Gershwin knew her, too, for she starred in his musical *Oh, Kay!*

Born practically in a theatrical trunk in London, where her parents performed in the music halls, at the age of ten (on the strength of a fortune-telling machine which predicted stardom for her) she had cards printed to announce "Little Gertie Lawrence, Child Actress and Danseuse."

She proved as able, touching and gripping in straight plays as in musicals. She never had a failure.

EVA LE GALLIENNE

WHEN Eva Le Gallienne was playing in Chicago in Molnár's *The Swan* during the Twenties, she remembers her mother standing in front of the Blackstone Theatre there, gazing at a large "blow-up" of Muray's famous picture of Eva as Princess Alexandra in that play. Mme. Le Gallienne had not seen her daughter in this role, as she was seldom in the U.S., and she exclaimed in amazement, "Why, you actually look beautiful!" Her mother never had any illusions as to Eva's looks.

Eva replied, "But Alexandra *is* beautiful."

And Eva Le Gallienne was and is one of the great luminaries of the American theater and the undisputed first lady of serious American repertory.

British-born in 1899, French-educated, Miss Le Gallienne first came to the United States in 1915 and was immediately adopted by us.

Her first great hit was scored as the sensitive, wistful and spiritual Julie in Molnár's *Liliom*, one of the early Theatre Guild productions, followed by *The Swan*. In 1926 she founded the Civic Repertory Theater, which during the next eight years presented some forty plays with Eva Le Gallienne participating as actress or director or both.

For the first time theatergoers became acquainted with Chekov in performances of *The Three Sisters*, *The Cherry Orchard* and *The Sea Gull*, as well as Jean Giraudoux. Represented in the repertory were Ibsen, Shakespeare, Dumas, Molière, Goldoni, the Quinteros, Sierra and Jean-Jacques Bernard. Two of the company's greatest hits were *Peter Pan* and *Alice in Wonderland*, with the latter accepted today as the standard translation of that wonderful and difficult-to-stage story into theater terms.

Today, at sixty-eight, Eva Le Gallienne is as vital and as busy as ever. A recent season found her touring for the National Repertory Theater, alternating the roles of Aurelia in *The Madwoman of Chaillot* and Hecuba in *The Trojan Women*.

BENNY LEONARD

HIS real name was Benjamin Leiner and, as you will note from the elegant silk dressing gown (prior to his times, pugs wore tattered bathrobes), he inaugurated the elite of boxing. With the advent of the Walker Law and the arrival of promoter Tex Rickard upon the scene, prize fighting became respectable—so respectable, in fact, that a society woman of the caliber of Miss Anne Morgan could promote a championship fight for charity. The opponents in Miss Morgan's show were Benny Leonard and Lew Tendler, and Leonard successfully defended his lightweight title in a classic and memorable brawl.

In 1925 Leonard retired as undefeated lightweight champion, ranked by many boxing experts as one of the greatest 135-pounders of all time.

Although he came from one of those tough East Side neighborhoods where a Jewish boy had to learn how to use his fists in order to survive, Leonard grew up into the first of that new breed of pugilists characteristic of the times—slick, smooth, soft-spoken, intelligent and wealthy. For the first time prize fighters were making money, and Leonard's battles with the left-handed Tendler drew gates in excess of $100,000, a startling figure at the beginning of the era. Yet before the decade was out we were to see Gene Tunney, the heavyweight champion of the world, paid a million dollars for a ten-round fight out of gate receipts of $2,658,660.

Leonard won his lightweight title in 1917, when he knocked out Freddy Welsh in nine rounds. Thereafter, it might be said, no one hit him hard or often enough to muss his hair in some thirty-six defenses of his title, in which he stiffened thirty of his challengers.

In 1931, alas, he began a comeback as a welterweight which ended in Madison Square Garden the night that Jimmy McLarnin stopped him in six rounds. I was there. He was only a memory of the old Benny Leonard. It was to weep.

SINCLAIR LEWIS

PRACTICALLY at the same time that the United States produced its first genuine suburban *bourgeoisie*, novelist Sinclair Lewis all but undermined it.

Before, with Little Jack Horner, we had a chance to say, "What a good boy am I," Red Lewis with such novels as *Main Street, Babbitt, Arrowsmith, Elmer Gantry, The Man Who Knew Coolidge* and *Dodsworth*, all published between 1920 and 1930, showed up the new civilization of which we were so proud as arid, vapid and phony, and us as repressed and bumbling hypocrites in love, in politics, in business and in life.

Main Street added to the self-awareness of the American people, and *Babbitt* added a word to their language—the name of its hero, George Babbitt. In the former novel Lewis satirized the superficiality of life in the Middle West. But the criticism reached to every part of the nation—New York and Los Angeles were full of Middle Westerners.

You could say of a neighbor, "He's a Babbitt," or "George Babbitt to the life, isn't he?" Though his business deals were just this side of being shady, Babbitt considered them patriotic contributions; he belonged to the right church, the right golf club, the right political party; he joined the Rotary Clubs and lodges, waved the flag, voted dry and drank wet. *Arrowsmith* satirized the medical profession; *Elmer Gantry* attacked the hypocrisy of the clergy.

There was a bit of Babbitt in all of us, a touch of Arrowsmith in our doctors and a lot of Elmer Gantry in our churches.

Red was a Middle Western boy himself, from Sauk Center, Minnesota, and in his case an unsuccessful newspaper career in San Francisco and New York not only got the boy out of the country but got the country out of the boy. He was one of the few American novelists who have had a genuine influence upon their times, and in 1930 he was awarded the Nobel Prize for Literature. He died in Rome in 1951 at the age of sixty-five, in a clinic and alone except for the Franciscan nursing sisters.

WALTER LIPPMANN

WALTER LIPPMANN, who writes as through a trumpet from Olympus on high, was once a young man.

He was born in 1889, and more has been forgotten about the career of the intense sitter facing the Muray lens than can be remembered of his early post-Harvard days when he was a frequenter of the famous salon of Mabel Dodge, to whose "evenings" on lower Fifth Avenue came the new intellectuals: Lincoln Steffens, John Reed, Carl Van Vechten, Jo Davidson, Harry Kemp the tramp poet, Frank Harris and Alan Seeger. According to Allen Churchill's book *The Improper Bohemians* "young Harvard socialists like Walter Lippmann argued with Bohemian socialists like Max Eastman." And America's most revered and dignified political philosopher of today appears enshrined in the following Greenwich Village lyric:

> Kemp thunders anarchism, and is wrecked
> On a sharp flint from Lippmann's intellect—
> Who Socialism in turn expounds . . .
> Seeger and Kemp each twangs his lyric lute
> And Poetry disdainfully dispute.

Today's philosopher and historian was formerly an editor, anonymously hidden behind the columns of the most sparkling newspaper of the day, the old New York *World*, to which Herbert Bayard Swope brought him in 1923, and where his lively mind was reflected in its columns. He remained until the great newspaper, one of the first of the vanishing metropolitan press to die, was merged with the *Evening Telegram*. Some of the most famed newspapermen in the history of American journalism worked for him: Heywood Broun, James M. Cain, Franklin P. Adams and Arthur Krock. The *World* perished from lack of financial blood supply to its brains. Hearst and Patterson were draining away circulation; rising mechanical costs cut profits. Lippmann came out from behind editorial anonymity and drew forth his pen like a shining sword.

Ever since his graduation from Harvard in 1910, along with such classmates as T. S. Eliot, Van Wyck Brooks, Conrad Aiken, Lee Simonson, Robert Edmond Jones and Alan Seeger, he has been a part of the intellectual growth of the United States, as at home in Europe and European politics as in America.

CISSIE LOFTUS

IN this study of Cissie Loftus, taken circa 1925, when she was forty-nine years of age, Muray seems to have penetrated to the tragedy that came close to wrecking one of the most fabulous lives of the British and American stage.

In 1923, having vanished inexplicably from the theater for ten years, she appeared in a London court on a narcotics charge, a wreck of the glorious person she had once been. She told how, compelled to seek relief from pain after the premature birth of a child, she had become addicted. She was placed on probation for a year and somehow in that time managed to conquer drugs.

Returning to the United States, she scored a sensational and emotional comeback at the old Palace Theatre, the home of vaudeville, where, after her twenty-minute act of impersonations, the house rose to its feet—many of those present in tears—and gave her an ovation which kept her on stage for more than an hour.

But Cissie was more than a mimic, although at the age of fifteen she was earning $2,000 a week in the London music halls with her mimicry, which included an impersonation of Sarah Bernhardt so exquisite that the great French actress herself congratulated Cissie after a performance.

Born in Glasgow in 1876, the daughter of two variety artists, Cissie Loftus was a star of stars. A few years after all London was roaring with laughter at her imitations of current actors and actresses, she turned to the legitimate stage and was sharing program billing with Sir Henry Irving, Ellen Terry, William Faversham, E. H. Sothern and Sarah Bernhardt herself.

Sir Arthur Sullivan considered it a privilege to accompany her at the piano and tried to persuade her her to abandon the stage for opera, for she had a lovely singing voice. Her greatest impact here came during the Twenties, when she scored triumph after triumph in such plays as *Diplomacy* and *Becky Sharp*.

ANITA LOOS

THE year was 1909 when a dark-haired, diminutive child actress and high-school student in San Diego, California, thought she had an idea for a moving picture. She wrote an outline entitled *The New York Hat*, addressed it to the manager of the Biograph Studios, New York City, and sent it off. She had seen a number of the early flickering films and found them pretty silly. In fact, she thought she could do better. She could, too. Then sixteen, she had been writing scenarios since she was twelve.

Busy with attending high school during the day and performing in her father's traveling melodramas, the R. Beers Loos Company, the young lady, Anita by name, forgot all about *The New York Hat* until one day she received a check for $15 from Biograph and a demand for more scenarios. Miss Loos obliged.

In New York, David Wark Griffith picked *The New York Hat* out of the pile at Biograph and shot it with Mary Pickford and Lionel Barrymore. Before long Anita was sent for by Griffith to come to Biograph as resident scriptwriter. She worked for him for five years, turning out a story a week. Then she wrote for Douglas Fairbanks and Constance Talmadge.

Anita Loos literally grew up with motion pictures, but pictures grew with and because of her as well, for she became the founder of the then undeveloped art of film titling. John Emerson, an actor whom she later married, pointed out to Griffith that he was throwing away the best feature of the young girl's scenarios, her clever, wise-cracking lines. Why not put them on the screen?

Yet her real fame came in 1925, when, to overcome the boredom of the ride out to Hollywood on The Chief, she described the doings of a little gold-digging actress called Lorelei Lee in a short novel entitled *Gentlemen Prefer Blondes*, which went into forty editions, was turned into a smash-hit play, movie and finally musical, became a best-seller in thirteen languages and made Miss Loos one of the celebrities of our times.

Of an encounter with Muray and his camera, Miss Loos writes: "I remember one time when I ran into Nick at a costume party. I was dressed in a child's outfit. Nick said I looked no more than twelve, though I was well over twenty, and insisted on making some pictures the next day, in this get-up. They were later seen by a movie director who demanded I play a schoolgirl in a film he was shooting. The day I walked onto the set to join a group of real children, one of the little boys piped up—'Look at *that* old girl! She must be a friend of the director.'"

MYRNA LOY

MOVING pictures go in cycles, as do heroes, heroines, villains, villainesses and vampires, except that the last-named is a thing of the past. If one appeared upon stage or screen today, she would only draw laughter. But in the Twenties she was very much with us, "the bad woman" who lured good men to their ruin. We believed in her as we did in Pear's Soap, Listerine, bucolic virtue, and sulphur-and-molasses in the springtime.

Nick Muray has here revealed Miss Myrna Loy, the screen actress, in the act of portraying the kind of female character that was supposed to produce the beast in us boys.

In 1927 one of her directors, Roy Del Ruth, wrote seriously of her: "In appearance she is startling —tall, graceful, with a grace acquired through years of dancing, titian-haired, with almond-shaped eyes as green as the sea and as baffling, eyes whose curling lashes shadow wisdom and mystery, and with these she used to work her will with those of the susceptible sex (we are speaking of her screen work, of course)."

Of course! For, actually, there couldn't have been a nicer or plainer kid than Myrna Williams, born on a cattle ranch in Raidersburg, Montana, where she grew up watching the cowpokes roping cattle and learned not to sit on a cactus plant.

After the death of her father, her family moved to California. She took up dancing at the Ruth St. Denis studio, and her first film role was a bit part in *Ben Hur*, given her after she modeled some costumes for a test of the dresses to be used in the film. Her name was changed to Loy by Rudolph Valentino and his wife, Natasha Rambova. She happened to strike a vogue of Oriental vampires and found herself playing Chinese, Polynesian, Filipino, Japanese, Malayan and Indian sirens.

Eventually, as tastes changed, she escaped from the vampire mold to star in more than two hundred films and become the screen wife of William Powell in the famous *Thin Man* series.

THE LUNTS

THE late Lawrence Langner, guiding genius of the Theatre Guild, in his book *The Magic Curtain* quotes an actress as complaining bitterly, "How can any other actors expect to play together as well as Alfred and Lynn? They rehearse in bed."

This comment serves to introduce the most enduring married couple in the American theater and one which over forty years has far outdistanced such well-known stage teams as Sir Henry Irving and Ellen Terry, or E. H. Sothern and Julia Marlowe. The Lunts still hold the center of the stage today, but they belong to the Twenties, for their first performance as husband and wife was in the celebrated Guild production of *The Guardsman* in 1924, the smash hit that made that company a financial success.

They had become famous before they were married: Lynn Fontanne as *Dulcy* in the play by George S. Kaufman and Marc Connolly out of a character from the column of Franklin P. Adams, and Alfred Lunt as *Clarence*, a part written especially for him by the popular American novelist Booth Tarkington.

Miss Fontanne, an English-born actress who, like so many, made her first appearance as a child in a Drury Lane pantomime, made Frank Adams' nitwit Dulcinea, the typical scatterbrained wife, a household name when she played her in New York in 1921 and then on tour. I remember her from that show as an extraordinary-looking creature possessed of a strange voice, sultry, drawling, ascending and descending. Girls of my day tried to talk like her, not too successfully.

Clarence made a celebrity of Milwaukee-born Alfred Lunt. When they were married in 1922, they did not plan to act together, but ever since *The Guardsman* they have formed the finest, most exciting, painstaking and successful pair in the theater.

For the rest of the decade we were never without a season of the Lunts on Broadway for the Guild, including *Arms and the Man, Goat Song, The Brothers Karamazov, The Doctor's Dilemma, Caprice* and *Elizabeth the Queen.*

CHARLES MACARTHUR

IN 1926–1927 Muray was living in a three-flight walk-up apartment at Lexington Avenue and 34th Street which he shared with Charles MacArthur. He took the bed during the night hours and Charlie used it during the day. The latter was working on the *Journal American*, a morning paper. At that time MacArthur had written two plays in collaboration: *Lulu Belle* and *Salvation*.

If irreverence signalized the postwar decade, Charlie MacArthur, cynical ex-Chicago and New York newspaper reporter, became its high priest and a stand-out character of the wacky period. His whirlwind courtship of Helen Hayes was part of the saga.

Muray claimed the legendary "Have-a-bag-of-peanuts-I-wish-they-were-emeralds" story happened in his studio. Seven other people insist it took place in theirs. One thing is certain: the pair became very fed up with the tale. Eventually Charlie topped it when he returned from the Eastern Theater of World War II with a bag of emeralds from India. He emptied them onto her palm with, "I wish they were peanuts."

MacArthur wanted a success as great as that of Miss Hayes. In her book, *A Gift of Joy*, Miss Hayes tells of the first night of *The Front Page*, that rapid-fire, wisecracking newspaper satire, with MacArthur and Ben Hecht, the co-author, sweating it out on the fire escape outside the theater while she herself sat in the balcony trembling. She wanted the play to be a smash, for she knew it would give her MacArthur. When Dorothy Stickney in the role of Mollie Malloy, the prostitute, stopped the show cold and received a ten-minute ovation after her exit, Helen ran to MacArthur, babbling hysterically that the play was a triumph. MacArthur's reply was, "Helen, will you marry me?"

BERNARR MACFADDEN

IT was at the beginning of our crowded and hysterical decade that a spate of new and horrible magazines appeared upon the news-stands, with lurid covers, absurdly amateur contents and such titles as *True Story, Love and Romance, Ghost Stories, True Detective, Master Detective, True Romances, True Experiences, Dream World*. Their publisher was one of the weirdest characters of that era. Born at Mill Springs, Missouri, in 1868, he struggled to preserve his body beautiful past the century mark, but finally gave up in 1955.

His name was Bernarr Macfadden, and through nourishing the moron element in the United States with advice on how to be strong, handsome and successful as well as a hand with the girls, he became a multi-millionaire publisher.

The accompanying picture was taken at Mr. Macfadden's request, as immortalized in Nick Muray's notes (see pages xxii-xxiii).

In my jobs on the *Daily News* I had to contend with the journalistic excesses of Mr. Macfadden's tabloid New York *Graphic*, which would stop at nothing, and piled on circulation with such coverage as he gave the famous Peaches Browning story.

This was the one in which an aging satyr by the name of Daddy Browning and a teenager called Peaches Heenan provided the first manifestation of Lolita-ism in the U.S. During their courtship, marriage, honeymoon and finally annulment suit, Bernarr Macfadden invented and front-paged the *Graphic* with something called a "composograph" which enabled him to show Mrs. Browning standing nude in front of the jury box, the picture being a composite of the body of a chorus girl with the head of Peaches pasted onto it and then re-photographed. Other composographs invaded the bath and nuptial chambers of the Brownings. Over on the *News* we could hardly wait for each next day's edition of *Graphic* to come off the presses.

PAUL MANSHIP

WHEN Nick Muray moved his portrait apparatus to the studio of Paul Manship around 1925, he captured not only the figure of one of America's greatest sculptors but also an enchanting example of Manship's work: the classic modeling, the airy movement, the combination of the ancient and the modern that was the earmark of the American renaissance.

Of Manship the late Royal Cortissoz, dean of American art critics, wrote: "Upon whatever he has done, he has flung a kind of impalpable veil that has made it good to look at, a thing to uplift the heart. The *Indian Hunter*, the *Dancer and Gazelles*, the statuette of a mother and her child, called *Playfulness*, and striding *Atalanta* and so on through a long list of enchanting works—what have these meant, if not a sculptor's magical insight into the mystery of form and his power of interpreting it in a beguiling silhouette?"

Again, he was among the Young Lochinvars who came out of the Midwest to carry off one of the Muses. Born in St. Paul, Minnesota, in 1885, he emigrated to the Pennsylvania Academy of Fine Arts, thence to the American Academy in Rome. He finally studied in the New York Studio of Solon Borglum, brother of Gutzon Borglum, creator of the famous Mount Rushmore National Memorial. Solon's specialty was the study of horses, and it was from him that Paul acquired his facility and delight in the delineation of animals.

From the time that Manship completed his studies until he died in 1966, he won practically every gold medal or prize for which he competed. He has left a legacy of stone and bronze, including the famous *Prometheus* surmounting the fountain in Rockefeller Center, the Paul Rainey Memorial· Gateway at the Bronx Zoo, the soldier's Monument at Thiaucourt in France, and busts of John D. Rockefeller, Jr., Woodrow Wilson and John Barrymore, besides statues and commemorative medals.

CYRIL MAUDE

SOME actors build up fame over the years in a series of characterizations which impress their personalities upon the public. Others achieve a lasting reputation by means of one play or one appearance which leaves its mark upon a generation.

Although Cyril Maude was seen on the New York stage in 1923 with Alma Tell and Leslie Howard in *Aren't We All?* and again in 1925 in a play by Michael Arlen, *These Charming People*, he is best remembered for an earlier characterization as Andrew Bullivant, a crusty old curmudgeon, in *Grumpy*, the play in which he toured both the United States and Canada.

When he died in 1951 at the age of eighty-eight, the anonymous author of his obituary in the London *Times* wrote: "Playgoers of long memory will testify to the many hours of pleasure conferred upon them by the air of happiness that radiated from Cyril Maude. No matter how bad-tempered the character he was assuming, his personal charm and familiar mannerism came through and it was plain that he was immensely enjoying his work and his success in his profession."

When he was born in London in 1862, the Civil War was raging in America, and by the time he appeared in *Grumpy* in New York, World War I was imminent and he already had behind him a long and successful career in Britain as not only an actor but actor-manager at the famous Haymarket Theatre. He appeared there in innumerable plays—*The Second Mrs. Tanqueray*, *The Little Minister*, *Cousin Kate*, *The Monkey's Paw* and Restoration comedies such as *She Stoops to Conquer*, *The Rivals* and *The School for Scandal*.

Maude was in his early sixties when Muray made this study of him during one of his runs on Broadway, but the unquenchable youth and quizzical humor that so delighted his audiences shine through.

NEYSA MCMEIN

THIS lovely-looking woman was a painter, a portraitist and a cover artist, and could herself have posed for one of the American girls with which she decorated the popular magazines.

She was also a short-story writer and one of the celebrities of our times. If you didn't know or hadn't met Neysa McMein, you weren't "in," and if you had had your portrait painted by her, you were most definitely of the elite. For among her sitters were Jack Dempsey, President Harding, Chief Justice Charles Evans Hughes, Charlie Chaplin, the Rev. Francis P. Duffy, Jascha Heifetz and Bea Lillie.

Another émigrée to New York from that seething caldron of talent, the Midwest, Miss McMein was born in Quincey, Illinois, earned her way through the Chicago Art Institute, worked in Chicago and came to New York in 1913. Two years later she sold her first cover to *The Saturday Evening Post*, and by the time the Twenties had dawned she had popularized the McMein Girl, just as during an earlier generation Charles Dana Gibson had created his famous Gibson Girl.

Prior to her advent, the magazines featured doll faces. Miss McMein painted attractive, smart-looking, high-bred American girls, and soon they were appearing not only on the *Post*, but on *Woman's Home Companion*, *Collier's* and *McCall's*.

It is hard to overestimate the influence of those magazines upon us. Stories, advertising and art all contributed to the American myth—life was a fairytale of happy endings, all men and women were beautiful and Prince Charming was just around the corner.

Describing the type of girl she drew, Miss McMein once said, "I didn't invent her, nor did I try to idealize her. I just take a pretty girl and draw her as she is."

The fallacy of the times, however, was that the plain girl never made the cover spot.

THOMAS MEIGHAN

FEW may recognize his picture today, but when I was a young man he was part and parcel of my consciousness. Tommy Meighan, motion-picture star! It is only when I look through volumes of old plays or movies that I realize the tremendous influence of the silent films. For I seem to have seen them all and know them all, and I can still remember Tom Meighan, how he looked and how he played, in a picture directed by Cecil B. DeMille entitled *Male and Female.*

Mr. DeMille didn't trust us, and probably rightly so, to be familiar with Sir James Barrie's *The Admirable Crichton,* which provided the story for *Male and Female.* Tommy Meighan played the butler cast away on a desert island with the rich girl and her family and the pathetic maid Tweeney who loved him. As he brought about the humbling of the haughty heiress and showed that beneath his butler's buttons beat the heart of a man and a hero, it was all so real to me I didn't even know I was sitting in on a socialist tract.

Thomas Meighan, who died in 1936 at the age of fifty-seven, was one of the few veteran actors who successfully made the transition from Broadway to the silent pictures. In silent films he was best known for his performance in *The Miracle Man.*

Born in Pittsburgh, Meighan, the square-jawed, clean-cut American type, for ten years from 1916 through 1927 was top box office, playing opposite leading ladies of the caliber of Billie Burke, Pauline Frederick, Norma Talmadge, Elsie Ferguson and Mary Pickford. Cutting their film teeth with him in subsidiary roles in his pictures were such feature stars as Myrna Loy, Bill Powell, Lynn Fontanne and Victor Moore.

PHILIP MERIVALE

WHAT is it that makes a matinee idol, that icing on the theatrical bun which packs theaters twice a week for afternoon performances when women come to give their libidos a vicarious work-out via some particular actor?

To be born British helps. Having a cleft chin and being handsome in an appealing way to awaken a cosy combination of desire coupled with a maternal instinct is better. Giving a smooth, suave, urbane performance, always under control, is yet another ingredient, and rumors of a flaming real-life romance tops him off. Philip Merivale combined all of these, and whenever he performed, long lines of Helen Hokinson's old girls would wind around the block from the ticket window.

The uniform here identifies the year and the play in which the late Philip Merivale was appearing when he posed for Muray. It was 1923 and he had a lead in Molnár's *The Swan*, opposite Eva Le Gallienne. In 1924 he was seen with that exquisite comedienne Ina Claire in *Grounds for Divorce;* in 1927 he portrayed Hannibal in Robert Sherwood's first play, *The Road to Rome*, with Jane Cowl; and in 1929 he appeared in *Death Takes a Holiday*. By 1933, when he played Bothwell with Helen Hayes in Maxwell Anderson's *Mary of Scotland*, he was one of the biggest box-office draws of Broadway.

And the great romance was with the beautiful English actress Gladys Cooper, whom he married after playing opposite her in a number of productions.

Born in India in 1887, where his father was engaged in building a railroad, Merivale went to England and graduated from Oxford. He began his apprenticeship in the theater with Sir Frank Benson's company, in which he acted practically every small part in Shakespeare, and advanced further when he joined the company of Sir Herbert Beerbohm Tree, playing opposite temperamental Mrs. Pat Campbell. But the lady was not too temperamental to recognize the potentialities of a good leading man, and it was she who first brought him to New York in 1914 to perform with her in *Pygmalion*.

JO MIELZINER

THERE was, as noted, in our whirling decade an outcropping of boy wonders—youthful geniuses in the various arts who grew up into the great creators of the present.

One of these was Jo Mielziner. At the tender age of twenty-three he designed the sets for *The Guardsman*, that milestone of a play we have already encountered as one of the standouts of the golden era. He was still a very young man when he designed the settings for *Strange Interlude*, *Street Scene* and *The Barretts of Wimpole Street*, but he was already a celebrity. Up to now he has worked on more than 250 productions since 1924, and all of them were based on his own axiom of his profession: "An actor must be *in* a set, not in front of a set."

It was only when our theater began its growth from puerile diversion to entertainment of consequence that the designer even began to be noticed, emerging from the anonymity of a hack who daubed a woodland scene onto canvas to an artist whose work would be reviewed by the dramatic critic.

Born in Paris in 1901, Jo Mielziner came to New York in 1909 and at the age of fifteen won a scholarship to the Pennsylvania Academy of Fine Arts. After a hitch in the U.S. Marines at Parris Island, he studied the European theater for two years and then, returning to New York in 1923, joined the Theatre Guild as a bit player and assistant stage manager. He continued his studies of painting and stage lighting under Lee Simonson. It was during this apprenticeship on both sides of the footlights that Mielziner learned the total technique of his craft, which was to create illusion in aid of the script, not only with paint and perspective but also with light, and he is today one of the greatest lighting experts in the world.

MARILYN MILLER

CERTAIN performers of the stage or screen have the unique ability of impressing their personalities upon their times so that the two appear to be indivisible. Marilyn Miller belonged to the Twenties as much as the Twenties belonged to her. An exquisite little creature who tragically died from a toxic illness in 1936 at the age of thirty-seven, she made her way into the hearts of her generation in the musical play *Sally*, which opened at the New Amsterdam Theatre in December 1920.

In 1924 she was *Peter Pan;* in 1925, *Sunny;* in 1928, *Rosalie;* and her last production of the decade was *Smiles*, at the Ziegfeld Theatre in 1930.

I saw her when she appeared in *Sally*. I can no longer recall what the play was about, but there lingers a memory of this charming figure dancing and trilling her way through something light, gay and frothy. There was no great singing voice there; she was not even an extraordinary ballerina; but she had the exuberant and delectable quality of eternal and unquenchable youth. She was so lovely she made one's heart ache.

With her, I seem to remember, was an extraordinary tap dancer by the name of Jack Donohue, a big, gangling, loose-limbed Irishman whose bizarre, craggy countenance and grace of performance were the forerunner of Ray Bolger. The simplicity of Donohue's style and his precision taps were a foil for Miss Miller, swirling in a pink tutu; it was beauty and the beast, and strangely touching.

She was one of those extraordinarily scintillating creatures who could communicate. Lee Shubert saw her dance one night at an entertainment at the Lotus Club, an association of musicians, writers and theatrical people, and engaged her for a small part in one of his Winter Garden shows. Florenz Ziegfeld engaged her for a fleeting number in his *Ziegfeld Follies of 1918*. She was on for hardly more than two or three minutes, but everyone in the theater was aware of star quality. Two years later she was *Sally* and a part of theatrical tradition of the Twenties.

FERENC MOLNÁR

FERENC MOLNÁR was our first Hungarian playwright. Any Hungarian is likely to be an experience, but the impact of Hungary's greatest writer cum *bon viveur* and conversationalist was earth-shaking, and was based upon four hit plays produced between 1920 and 1930: *Liliom*, *The Guardsman*, *The Play's the Thing* and *The Swan*. No little of his reputation was based on the personality he brought to his adopted city, New York, where he died in 1952.

Budapest-born in 1878, a journalist, essayist and indefatigable raconteur, he was first introduced to America, oddly enough, in 1908 in New York, when four companies were simultaneously performing one of his first plays, *The Devil*—two of the productions were in English, one in German, and the fourth one in Yiddish at the old Irving Place Theatre. He was then forgotten here for twelve years until in 1921 the Theatre Guild produced *Liliom*.

Liliom had a curious history in the theater. It was supposed to have been written in Budapest by Molnár as he sat at a café table, half listening to the ubiquitous and inevitable gypsy band. It opened there in 1901 and was a complete failure.

When, in the Forties, Lawrence Langner suggested that Rodgers and Hammerstein make a musical of this touching story of the gangster who after death came back to the girl he had abandoned, Molnár refused his permission. Langner begged him to see *Oklahoma!* Molnár went and, returning full of excitement, declared that if his play could get the same treatment from Rodgers and Hammerstein, he would consent. *Carousel* was the result.

In 1940 Molnár exiled himself from Hungary when the Nazis moved in. He became a well-known figure around Central Park South, where he lived but never acclimated. His heart always yearned for his raffish and witty cronies in the sidewalk cafés of old Budapest.

CLAUDE MONET

IF an era or a decade can be known for those who lived through it, it may be equally distinguished for a great personage who chose it in which to die, particularly such a giant as Claude Monet, who on December 5, 1926, looked for the last time at his home at Giverney, at the light and air whose aspects he was so successful in transferring to canvas.

Thanks to men like Frank Crowninshield, one was already familiar with the French Impressionist school. There had been that Armory Exhibition in 1913, reproductions in *Vanity Fair* and other magazines, so that we had acquaintance with the names not only of Monet, but of Renoir, Sisley, Cézanne, Degas and Manet.

Monet reaches back into what, for us, is almost ancient history: the France in which Napoleon had been dead for no more than nineteen years, for Monet was born in Paris in 1840. His lifetime's output of pictures, today worth into the millions of dollars, speaks for itself. But what is forgotten is the unquenchable and indomitable honesty and nobility of spirit inhabiting the frame of the old gentleman here standing in his garden as he waits for the photographer to prepare to click the shutter, unaware—as Muray wrote—that picture after picture was being shot.

As a young man he had entered the studio of Gleyre, a classicist who tried to force him into the strait-jacket of conventional art and away from truth, warning Monet never to produce nature as he saw it, but always to think of the antique.

Two of Monet's fellow students were Sisley and Renoir, to whom the young rebel said, "Let's clear out of here; the atmosphere is unwholesome; there's a lack of sincerity."

The three abandoned the studio, and each went his own way to paint whatever he saw and felt in terms of light and color, and the school of Impressionism had its impetus. But Monet had to struggle for twenty years before his artistic concepts began to gain acceptance.

COLLEEN MOORE

THE affinities between the inhabitants of this volume continue. F. Scott Fitzgerald described the flapper; John Held, Jr., drew her; Colleen Moore brought her to life for the first time in *Flaming Youth* for First National Pictures in 1923, starting a vogue which led her to become the highest-paid screen actress of those times. She earned a salary of $12,500 per week, which, in terms of the unhappy devaluation of the dollar bill over the last forty years, would be equal to more than $100,000 today. Scott Fitzgerald wrote of her: "I was the spark that lit up flaming youth, Colleen Moore was the torch. What little things we are to have caused all that trouble."

Who and what were flappers? How did they flap? They had thin legs like sticks which, when they Charlestoned, waved like semaphores; no breasts; short-cropped hair; a slouch. They were addicted to long-stemmed cigarette holders, a drink called a "Pink Lady" and necking. Sometimes when the "Pink Ladies" and the necking worked in too close combinations, the flapper woke up to find that she was no longer a virgin, though a flapper still, for that was a part of the revolt of the Twenties. Clara Bow played her for sex; Colleen Moore, for a romp—youth for the first time free to have its fling and assert its individuality.

Born in 1902 as Kathleen Morrison, she was renamed Colleen Moore by none other than D. W. Griffith, a friend of her family, when he visited them in Chicago and first saw her potentialities. In 1918 she was an extra at the Essanay studio; five years later came *Flaming Youth*, and from then on she was a part of the era and the symbol of its madcap, happy-go-lucky youngsters who refused to take either themselves or anybody else seriously. The titles of some of her subsequent pictures indicate the mold into which she was cast: *Painted People, The Perfect Flapper, Ella Cinders, It Must Be Love, Orchids and Ermine, Naughty But Nice* and *Her Wild Oat.*

GRACE MOORE

A MONOGRAPH remains to be written on the dangers of the church choir to impressionable and ambitious young girls who first raise their fresh lyric voices not far from the organ. Somebody comments after the service, "My, what a pretty voice your daughter's got!" And the trouble begins.

It was the First Baptist Church in Jellico, Tennessee, where Grace Moore was soloist at the evening services. One day in Nashville she heard Mary Garden sing, went backstage, threw her arms about her and swore that someday she, too, would be an opera star.

The returns for a long time were negative. Her teachers were doubtful, the critics unkind, and Artur Bodanzky, the chief conductor at the Metropolitan, told her bluntly, "No matter how hard you work, you'll never become an opera singer."

Her family objected to her musical career. Grace ran away to Greenwich Village and warbled in a cabaret.

Miss Moore entered our decade when, in 1920, she appeared with the comedian Raymond Hitchcock in something called *Hitchy-Koo*. Irving Berlin, who knew a voice when he heard one even if the critics did not, starred her in his *Music Box Revues* of 1923 and 1924, and the former choir singer was firmly established.

At the height of her popularity in musical comedy, in early March of 1926, she sailed to Europe to study opera. Giulio Gatti-Casazza, impresario of the Metropolitan, heard her sing in Milan. In 1928 she made her debut in New York as Mimi, and the little choir girl from Jellico gave our marvelous decade another jolt. With the Governor of Tennessee, George M. Cohan, Irving Berlin and Otto Kahn cheering her on, she was an opera star.

In the Thirties she acquired yet another triumph in moving pictures. Her death at the age of forty-five in a flaming plane crash in Copenhagen was one of the stunning tragedies of 1947.

MIKHAIL MORDKIN

AN odd way to take a shot at someone, but then that was ballet, and the archer was Mikhail Mordkin, Russian dancer, a member of Serge Diaghilev's Ballet Russe de Monte-Carlo, featuring such immortals as Nijinsky, Pavlova, Karsavina and Fokine.

The Diaghilev group, which for the first time exported the great Russian dance art to Europe and thence to America, was unquestionably responsible for the acceptance of the classic dance in the New World. Our cultural education has always depended upon showmen, showmanship, great performers and publicity. It took an eccentric onetime Russian lawyer and impresario, Diaghilev, to make Americans aware of the extraordinary merits of Nijinsky, whose leaps in *Spectre de la Rose* verged on the mystery of levitation, and his partner, Pavlova.

The nineteenth-century Americano was content to accept what he called toe dancers, but young men leaping about in tight pants or leopard skins were likely to bring forth catcalls. The reaction against male dancers was instinctive. Diaghilev and men like Nijinsky and Mordkin changed all that.

Mordkin had appeared with Anna Pavlova at the Metropolitan Opera House in 1910 with great success. After returning to Russia and nearly losing his life in the Bolshevist revolution, he came back to a succeeding generation in 1924.

When a definitive history of the development of the American musical is written, it will be remembered not only as an indigenous art form, but also as a haven for individuals in every performing profession. On his return to New York, Mordkin and his company of dancers, doing creative modern-jazz numbers, were presented in the fall edition of the famous *Greenwich Village Follies* at the Shuberts' Winter Garden, and ballet received a genuine impetus among the young.

ANNE MORGAN

THIS was one of the richest women in the world. She was also one of the finest, most courageous and most philanthropic, a combination which attracts less attention than fisticuffs in a night club, a runaway marriage or scandalous behavior in the upper echelons of stardom. Kindness and consideration for others do not make headlines.

The art of Nickolas Muray has never been more illuminated than by this portrait of a determined woman who all through her lifetime hated slowness and was impatient with stupidity. Completely self-effacing, she avoided publicity except when it was necessary for her causes. Then she met reporters with grim determination and usually, according to one newspaper interviewer compelled to face her, dictated her interview "through set teeth."

Born in New York in 1873, the daughter of J. Pierpont Morgan and sister of J. P. Morgan, the bankers whose incredible wealth was rivaled only by that of John D. Rockefeller, Miss Morgan spent herself and her fortune in repairing the insane ravages of two world wars. Frequently under fire in France during World War I, she was decorated with the Croix de Guerre with Palms, and the Légion d'Honneur.

The list of her philanthropic interests would fill a volume. She cared about the sailors in the Brooklyn Navy yard, about industrial and sanitary conditions surrounding women workers, about vacations for working girls, about American business and professional women, about child nurseries and dispensaries, health centers and public playgrounds. But her main contribution was the organization in 1917 of the American Committee for Devastated France, which even before the guns were silenced had found new living quarters for more than 50,000 homeless villagers, reconstructed more than 800 farms and provided rest houses that served some 45,000 soldiers and 4,000 refugees.

HELEN MORGAN

HER nickname when I knew her was "Mousie." Her specialty was perching on a piano in night clubs, where during the Prohibition era she introduced and sang sad, plaintive songs of longing or blighted love which were known as torch songs.

In those times, being in love, requited or un-, was called "carrying the torch for someone." One could not sit on a back fence and yowl one's heartache, but one could hole up in Helen Morgan's club, acquire a skinful of Prohibition hooch and leave it to Helen vicariously to sing one's blues in her wonderful, tearful, throaty, dark-colored voice.

We were too engaged with Marilyn Miller when she opened in Ziegfeld's *Sally* to notice a chorus girl named Helen Morgan in the same show. But in 1925, when she sang at the Back Stage Club, she climbed onto a piano to sing because the *boîte* had such a small, crowded floor that she had to get on a higher level to be seen. Thereafter she was never again unnoticed.

Her biggest hit was in Ziegfeld's *Show Boat*, the musical made from Edna Ferber's novel of Mississippi River floating theaters, and her most famous song was "My Bill," in which she lamented that though he was just an ordinary guy with not much to distinguish him, he was yet all hers. She made all of us feel like Bill.

Perhaps no other singer or character was more tied up with what we did and how we felt during that decade. For beneath our gaiety there must have lingered some guilt feeling, and if not that, then a sadness at something we were losing. Was this the catch in Mousie's throat or the sorrow in her expression—the turned-down mouth, the grieving eyes? Whatever, she was a lovely creature and a dear person and went away from us far too soon when she died in Chicago in 1941, at the age only of forty-one.

ALLA NAZIMOVA

NO one examining the photograph of the late Alla Nazimova in a 1918 film entitled *Eye for Eye* would imagine that this was "The Great Nazimova" of the past and the future, or find much hope for the silent flicks as an art form.

The foremost protagonist of Ibsen on the American stage is seen with a sash hoicked about her thighs, baring her legs, her midriff exposed, something shapeless binding her bosom, a jeweled band around her forehead, and against some kind of Turkish background she is waving a large snickersnee. A year later they have the same star dressed up as a Chinese girl in *The Red Lantern*.

One of the finest acting talents of our era continued to be miscast as a vampire, Oriental siren or tart until, in a desperate attempt to stem the tide of horrendous pictures which included a performance of *Camille* with Rudolph Valentino, in 1922 she quit Metro and produced her own version of *Salome* with sets designed from the drawings of Aubrey Beardsley. She scored an artistic success and a financial flop and lost her life savings. But the silly sequence of moronic films was broken.

A Russian actress, born in Yalta in 1879, she came to New York in 1905 to play Russian roles in Russian at the old Herald Square Theatre. The Shuberts saw her and offered her a contract if she could learn to speak English competently. A certain Mrs. Barthelmess taught her to speak in five months. Ten years later the teacher's son, Richard, had a small part when Nazimova made her screen debut in *War Brides*.

In 1928 her art became full-flowered when she turned her back on Hollywood and joined Eva Le Gallienne's Civic Repertory Theatre. In 1930 she first acted for the Theatre Guild, and from then on she went from triumph to triumph via Turgenev's *A Month in the Country*, O'Neill's *Mourning Becomes Electra* and her greatest role, Mrs. Alving in Ibsen's *Ghosts*.

PRINCE OBOLENSKY

IT is a pity that "Prince" Michael Romanoff, born Harry Gergusson in Brooklyn, never was brought to bay by the lens of Nick Muray as was Prince Alexis Alexandrovitch Obolensky. For Nick would then have run the gamut of our prince and royalty syndrome of the Twenties. With one hand the brash and irreverent tabloid the *Daily News* was, in its social columns, celebrating this former Czarist cavalry officer and genuine member of one of the oldest families of Russia. With the other, in its news columns it was exposing a series of pants-pressers, ex-bartenders and adventurers as "Quince Princes" and phony noblemen. Both kinds made headlines and were entertained by American society in palatial Long Island homes.

This imposing man was everything that a Russian prince ought to have been. His family had once owned more than a million and a quarter acres of land in the Urals and traced its ancestry back to one of the early Czars. He was educated at the Imperial University of St. Petersburg, commissioned and served throughout World War I in the Chevalier-Gardes, the crack cavalry regiment of the old Russian army. And it is remembered that during the campaigns, around the campfire, he sang for the bivouacked soldiers with a great, resounding bass voice—one which later proved to be his salvation, for recently his widow, the former Princess Troubetskoy, remarked, "We lived off his voice."

When during the revolution he escaped to Constantinople with his family and nothing but a Stradivarius and a string of pearls, he developed his singing, came to the United States to concertize and teach, and became a part of the New York scene and the musical world of his friends Damrosch, Zimbalist and Heifetz.

But, above all, he remained a prince—and was probably the only one ever officially to quit the union. For when some of his fellow Russian refugees of noble blood objected to his taking the part of a Soviet commissar in a Broadway musical show, he promptly resigned from the Russian Nobility Association, of which he had been president.

EUGENE O'NEILL

IN 1926, when Muray photographed the O'Neill family, Eugene O'Neill had already won two Pulitzer Prizes. Two years later he would accept a third, and eventually he would find himself the recipient of the Nobel Prize for Literature. With him in this photograph is the second of his three wives, Agnes Boulton. The playwright is holding Mrs. Charles Chaplin when she was baby Oona, and his arm is about the shoulders of his son Shane.

Eugene O'Neill was unquestionably the greatest contribution that the Twenties had to make to the stage, for it was during that decade that this strange, tortured man produced almost all of the plays which made him famous then and which will hold him equally famous generations from now.

In 1920 he was awarded his first Pulitzer Prize for *Beyond the Horizon*, in 1922 he received a second for *Anna Christie* and in 1928 a third for *Strange Interlude*.

During this same ten years he was writing classics such as *The Emperor Jones*, *The Hairy Ape*, *All God's Chillun Got Wings*, *Desire Under the Elms*, *Marco Millions*, *Mourning Becomes Electra* and, spilling over into the Thirties, *Ah, Wilderness!* and *Days Without End*. It was in 1936 that the creative impact of his plays won for him the Nobel Prize.

Has the camera caught defiance here? A look of a man who has overcome almost insuperable obstacles? O'Neill did; he was a onetime sailor, alcoholic and frequenter of the lowest waterfront dives, one of them a Village saloon known as The Working Girl's Home, where John Masefield was for a period employed as a bartender.

At one time O'Neill appeared to be pointing toward a sodden death in a gutter, but he pulled himself together and, as though some strange dam within had burst, poured forth a flood of the finest plays by any American dramatist.

ROSAMOND PINCHOT

THE life and death of Rosamond Pinchot form a strange and tragic tale. She was one of the most notable stage figures of the decade, but she was never an actress in the true sense of the word; she had every reason to live, yet she killed herself.

Rosamond Pinchot came from a socially prominent and famous family. Her uncle was Gifford Pinchot, one-time Governor of Pennsylvania. She was born in New York in 1906, went to all the right schools and was abroad with her mother in the summer of 1923, with not a single thought of ever going on the stage. She was then seventeen. Mother and daughter boarded the steamer *Aquitania* for the journey home, making plans for Rosamond's social debut that winter.

Three days out, a little Austrian theatrical manager, Max Reinhardt, was conferring on deck with his musical director and the German playwright Karl Vollmoeller, author of *The Miracle*, which Reinhardt was planning to produce in New York. They needed a young, tall, beautiful girl with the strength to walk the many miles on stage required by the movement of the Nun during each performance.

Reinhardt happened to look up as Rosamond Pinchot came swinging by. "*Du lieber Gott!*" he said. "It's the Nun!"

The success of the amateur Miss Pinchot in the first of some 750 performances of *The Miracle*, in which Lady Diana Manners played the Madonna, was one of the sensations of the theatrical season of 1924. She was then just going on nineteen.

Two years later she quit, yet the greasepaint had got into her blood, and in the spring of 1927 she joined the Reinhardt company again. At the age of twenty-three she married William Gaston, whose great-grandfather had been a Governor of Massachusetts. In 1936 she separated from her husband. In 1938 she shut herself in a car in her garage on an estate at Syosset, Long Island, led a tube from the exhaust pipe to her mouth, switched on the engine and died.

COLE PORTER

NO country in the world has been as prodigal of writers of popular music as America. But Cole Porter's lyrics and music were something special, indefinable in their appeal as well as in their ability to make an indelible imprint upon one's memory.

He might have been described as the Scott Fitzgerald of the musical world. No Tin Pan Alley song-plugger, he. Until a riding accident in 1937 forced him to become a recluse, he and his wife, the former Linda Lee Thomas of Louisville, Kentucky, lived a gay and lighthearted social life in Paris, on the Riviera and in Venice, as well as back home.

When the thousands gather in the Yale Bowl for the football games in the fall, not one in a hundred knows or remembers that when the cheerleaders urge them into singing "Bingo Eli Yale" or the "Yale Bulldog Song," they are performing words and music by Cole Porter, Yale graduate.

Irene Bordoni made her great American success with her arch and naughty rendition of Cole Porter's "Let's Do It." He was his own lyricist, and his marriages of words and music were extraordinarily felicitous and more than usually apt, for he had an ingenious and quirky mind.

During the early Twenties he was serving his apprenticeship for Broadway musicals, contributing songs to *Hitchy-Koo* and the *Greenwich Village Follies*. By the end of the decade he had written scores for *Paris, Wake Up and Dream* and *Fifty Million Frenchmen*, and thereafter he poured forth, practically up to his passing in 1964, a steady stream of melodies.

My life seems to have been lived to Cole Porter lyrics and tunes, such as "Night and Day," "What Is This Thing Called Love?," "Begin the Beguine" and "Love for Sale." Each one recalls some cycle or phase—where I was and what I was doing, where I was living. He was easy to sing and impossible to forget.

FLORENCE REED

IF you had been in New York in 1926, the theater would have offered you such riches as it had never before poured forth and probably not surpassed since.

There was *Broadway* with Lee Tracy, Gershwin's musical *Oh, Kay!*, with Gertrude Lawrence and Victor Moore, Lenore Ulric in *Lulu Belle*, Francine Larrimore and Dorothy Stickney in *Chicago* and Ethel Barrymore in *The Constant Wife*. You could see *What Every Woman Knows*, *Hedda Gabler*, *Cyrano*, *Ghosts* or Eugene O'Neill's *The Great God Brown*. The Lunts were teamed in *Goat Song;* F. Scott Fitzgerald's *The Great Gatsby* was on the boards, and so was *Gentlemen Prefer Blondes*. The police closed two plays, *The Captive*—the first attempt to depict lesbianism in the theater—and *Sex*, which brought overnight fame to Mae West, along with ten days in the cooler.

And it was also the year that Florence Reed scored her most sensational success as the Chinese brothel keeper, "Mother Goddam," in *The Shanghai Gesture*. She was also the first stage luminary ever to sit for Muray, of which near catastrophe Nick wrote:

"I was so nervous I almost wrecked the studio. It was early in my Village career and I was still using old-fashioned equipment in a confined space. Somehow to be in the same room with this magnificent and exotic creature made me all thumbs and left feet. Hustling about my camera, I knocked over a chair, almost kicked over the tripod and became inextricably tangled in the black focusing cloth to the point where I could have wept. A moment longer and I should have abandoned the entire project and run hysterically from the room, when Miss Reed, with the graciousness for which she was known, cried laughing, 'Don't worry, Mr. Muray, I know just how you feel. It's like me on a first night.'

"The tension relaxed and one of my favorite studies resulted."

ELMER RICE

O NE of the numerous condensed biographies of playwright of the Twenties Elmer Rice notes briefly: "Pre-theater lawyer," and his first play, which set him on the road to becoming one of the outstanding dramatists, was written and produced in 1914, two years after he had graduated *cum laude* from New York University Law School and been admitted to the bar. It was a courtroom drama called *On Trial*. And in connection with his occupation prior to becoming a dramatist, the late Mr. Rice liked to tell the following story:

"I had been a law clerk for some years and was making $15 a week (imagine that—a managing clerk and a member of the bar!) when I quit to write this play.

"Everybody said I was out of my mind, throwing up such a fine position. There was every prospect that in twenty years or so, with industry and good behavior, I'd be making $60 a week if I remained.

"I didn't have a cent in the world but still I wouldn't listen. I resigned and finished my play. It was accepted for production by Cohan and Harris. I knew nothing, absolutely nothing, about the theater. We went into rehearsal, and then came the tryout in Stamford, Connecticut.

"After the second act, George M. Cohan, who was one of the producers, and I stood smoking a cigarette in the lobby. Cohan said, 'Look here, kid, I'll give you $30,000 for your rights in this show.' He was in deadly earnest. I said no. If he had said $1,000, I would have jumped at it. I would have understood $1,000—just a little more than I had been making a year. But $30,000 was beyond my comprehension. I really didn't know there was such money or that anybody had it."

The musty law offices saw Elmer Rice no more, and between 1919 and 1930 he wrote or collaborated upon *For the Defense*, *The Adding Machine*, *The Subway* and his most famous play, *Street Scene*, for which he received the Pulitzer Prize in 1929.

HUGO RIESENFELD

THE impact of this scholarly violinist, musicologist and conductor from Vienna upon the Twenties was a curious one. Old-timers will remember him for his presentation at the Rialto Theatre, at Broadway and 42nd Street, of a musical mélange he called "classical jazz," which was the pop music of the day given the scoring and attention of a full symphony orchestra. But his really significant contribution was to help the movies grow up musically.

Whereas classical jazz was a have-your-cake-and-eat-it novelty which appealed to the middle-brows of our times, the marriage of Tin Pan Alley and Philharmonia, while it might have outraged the longhairs, gave the patrons of the famous Broadway movie house the feeling that they were absorbing culture as well as having fun. Dr. Riesenfeld pioneered the musical accompaniment of films, spending months at selecting an appropriate score of good music played by a good orchestra to enhance the features shown in his three theaters: the Rialto, the Rivoli and the Criterion.

One of the strange phenomena of the earliest motion-picture presentation, the nickelodeon set up in a store, was that it never occurred to anyone to let them unreel in silence. At the very least a pianist ad-libbed an accompaniment to the agonies endured upon the screen over his head. There was excitement music, burglar music, ghost music and, when things got really emotional, "Hearts and Flowers." Often there was a drummer as well, who could produce galloping hoofs, pistol shots and gunfire.

With the coming of the long feature film in the great entertainment palaces of Broadway, the modest Viennese musician chose music he felt fitting to the action of the scene from composers of all ages, blending it into a score. He always kept to the idea that the audience should be unconscious of the music and yet at the same time subconsciously affected by it, so that they would feel the impact of the film more strongly. Scores for today's pictures are specially composed, but it was Dr. Riesenfeld who made the transition.

PAUL ROBESON

IT took a genius to breach the national wall of Negro prejudice, and Paul Robeson, Princeton-born son of a Negro minister who had been a runaway slave and a mother who was two-thirds American Indian, was that genius.

In 1898, when Paul first saw the light of day, not much was said or done about the issue of civil rights, equal opportunity for the colored races, integration of schools. Robeson's contribution to bringing these about was to be himself, a Negro of such unusual attainments that he became a national figure. He was a star athlete, a Phi Beta Kappa, a concert singer, an actor, a lawyer, a professional football player, one of the most telling Othellos ever to appear upon the stage and, by the life he lived and his accomplishments, one of the greatest spokesmen for his people.

At Rutgers University he won twelve letters in athletics (four in football, three in baseball, three in basketball, two in track), was chosen for Walter Camp's All-America football squad and was a star on the debating team as well. Upon graduation he was voted one of the four seniors who best represented the ideals and traditions of Rutgers.

He took his law degree at Columbia University, but we knew him best as an actor for New York's Provincetown Players, where he was a member of the group that included Eugene O'Neill, Emma Goldman, Heywood Broun, Alexander Woollcott and Carl Van Doren. He appeared in such plays as *Tabu* and Eugene O'Neill's *The Emperor Jones* and *All God's Chillun Got Wings*. George Jean Nathan wrote, "Robeson, with relatively little experience, and with no training to speak of, is one of the most thoroughly eloquent, impressive and convincing actors I have looked at and listened to in almost twenty years of theater-going." His appearance on the concert stage as a basso singing Negro spirituals was equally sensational.

In this moving study Nick Muray has captured both the power and the melancholy of Paul Robeson.

EDWARD G. ROBINSON

WHEN this photograph was shown to that remarkable Rumanian, Edward G. Robinson, with the query as to what he might have been doing at the time he posed for it, he said, "Oh yes, that was my Smith & Wesson period."

Eddie Robinson has been a star and a personality for so long that he belongs not to any one period, but rather to the last half-century, which he has consistently decorated with one outstanding performance after another.

What he was referring to as his "Smith & Wesson" period was his portrayal of gangsters. He appeared onstage in *The Racket* and "Scarsi" in *Chicago*, and in films as the thug in *Little Caesar* in 1930, which dramatized the character of Al Capone and started an entire cycle of Prohibition hoodlum pictures. All through the Twenties, Robinson was never off the Broadway stage, appearing in every kind of role from comedy to melodrama to the classics.

He was one picture actor who was not at a loss when the silent movies began to talk. He could—in nine languages. During World War II he was in England, broadcasting in all of them to the European underground. It was his second war; in the first he served in the United States Navy.

Of all the Hollywood film colony, he is probably the most cultured: linguist, wit, musician, painter, collector of art and one of the first to recognize the impact of the French Impressionists; his house in Beverly Hills is still filled with them.

He was born in Bucharest in 1893 to Morris and Sarah Goldenberg, who emigrated to the United States in 1903, at which point Emanuel, as he had been christened, began the business of becoming an American by graduating from Townsend Harris High School and Columbia University. He wears the ribbon of a Chevalier de la Légion d'Honneur of France.

RODGERS AND HART

THERE were a number of ways you could acquire your non-athletic insignia at Columbia University, the silver King's Crown watch charm, and one of them was to serve as press agent to the Varsity Show. Having won my letter at crew, I elected to try for the King's Crown in 1921, my senior year, by selling the merits of the Varsity Show, which was to run for a week at the Astor Hotel, to the downtown press. It wasn't difficult, since all I had to exploit was two budding geniuses, Richard Rodgers and Lorenz Hart.

Broadway was not yet aware of this pair that, before the decade was out, would have revolutionized the American musical with such shows as *The Garrick Gaieties*, *Dearest Enemy*, *The Girl Friend* and *A Connecticut Yankee*. But we on Morningside Heights knew, because this was their second Varsity Show collaboration and there had not been such a campus combination in years. Music poured from Dick Rodgers, poetry from Lorenz Hart.

They were already famous when they faced Muray's camera, but still boy wonders and looking as they had when they were to be found on Columbia's asphalt campus. Larry Hart, the older, was doing post-graduate work, but when I first saw Dick Rodgers he was wearing the freshman's obligatory little black skullcap. And he was the first freshman ever to compose the Varsity Show.

The partnership was to continue into the Forties with such superb efforts as *On Your Toes*, *Babes in Arms*, *I Married an Angel*, *The Boys from Syracuse* and the famous *Pal Joey*, which set new standards for the American musical as a genuine indigenous art form. Little Larry Hart, who, according to Oscar Hammerstein, "skipped and bounced around the stage like an electrified gnome", died of pneumonia at the age of forty-seven. Thereafter the era of Rodgers and Hammerstein was inaugurated.

Today Dick Rodgers, the kid from Columbia, is America's finest living composer.

FRANKLIN D. ROOSEVELT

THIS was the face of the Democratic candidate for President of the United States in 1932, who a year later brought an end to the hangover and panic following upon the collapse after the great crash of '29, with his ringing admonition, "The only thing we have to fear is fear itself."

At the time this photograph was taken, Franklin Delano Roosevelt, an unusually young-appearing executive at the age of fifty, was Governor of the State of New York.

As Herbert Hoover had inherited the financial disaster at the end of the Twenties, Roosevelt fell heir to the shards that Hoover had not been able to reassemble, and our sins of the previous decade were truly visited upon him. The lens here has scored a rare penetration, for it looks within a man. For all of being but half a one, the muscles of his legs and lower abdomen paralyzed by infantile paralysis, he was capable of coping with the situation.

With the nation on the brink of disintegration, here is the leader who pulled it together with his inaugural address of 1933 and who stemmed the panic by closing the banks, embargoing gold and, by his eloquence, capturing the public imagination and succeeding indeed in banishing fear.

With clear-eyed courage and dispatch, he sent bills through Congress dealing with the banking crisis, the relief crisis, the agricultural crisis and many other problems, so that when Congress adjourned in June following his inauguration the practical rescue of the country from chaos had been accomplished.

He is remembered, of course, as our most famous war President and the only one, past, present or future, to be elected to a fourth term (since the law now limits the President to two terms). But this Franklin D. Roosevelt answered his country's cry for help not only in war, but in peacetime as well.

HAROLD ROSS

IF *Vanity Fair* was the incubator for the pre-sophisticates trying out their wings, then *The New Yorker* was an entire maternity hospital for the smart literary and graphic set that was to make an enduring name in the mid-Twenties. First published around St. Valentine's Day in 1925, it was the brain child of a Westerner, Harold Ross. His magazine was the first that ventured to sell the utmost in sophistication while barring the trite, the commonplace and the mediocre.

And what is more, Ross dared to say so in his prospectus, for which he wrote: "*The New Yorker* will be a reflection in word and picture of metropolitan life. . . . It will hate bunk. . . . *The New Yorker* will be a magazine which is not edited for the old lady in Dubuque. It will not be concerned with what she is thinking about. This is not meant in disrespect, but *The New Yorker* is a magazine avowedly published for a metropolitan audience and thereby will escape an influence which hampers most national publications. . . ."

There are people who will tell you New York is not America, but in many ways *The New Yorker* became the spokesman for the New America that was to stop taking itself so seriously and laugh its way into the Forties, Fifties and Sixties.

Ross, born in Aspen, Colorado, in 1892, was an itinerant newspaper reporter until World War I, when he became editor of the Army publication in France, *The Stars and Stripes*, whose staff included such notables as Alexander Woollcott, Frank Adams and Grantland Rice. In 1925, backed by Fleischmann yeast money, he sent his first *New Yorker* to press and thereby became one of the unique characters of the town. For it was a one-man magazine, and Ross, with his dislikes and foibles, his passion for the English language and good writing, was its sole arbiter and ran an utterly mad shop.

When in 1951 Ross died suddenly at the age of fifty-nine, his magazine had reached a circulation of over 400,000, two thirds of whom were *non-New Yorkers*.

HELENA RUBINSTEIN

THIS is the Princess Artchil Gourielli-Tchkonka, and the reason for the slightly self-satisfied smile upon her face is that under her maiden name, Helena Rubinstein, she parlayed a jar of face cream into a multimillion-dollar business. Before she died in 1965, at the age of ninety-four, she had become a world-famous figure and a living legend. Elizabeth Arden was her only real rival in the international cosmetics business.

The producer of that first jar of cream remains anonymous, described merely as a Hungarian physician who supplied it to the women of Helena's family. Later on, having studied medicine and chemistry, she made up her own creams, but the one on which her fabulous fortune was founded accompanied her in her baggage when she was shipped off to Australia by her family to get over an unhappy love affair.

Arrived Down Under and struck by the leathery skins of the settler's windblown wives, she ordered a shipment of the Hungarian face cream, accumulated $100,000 and in 1908 opened her first salon in London.

It was shortly before the advent of the Twenties that Miss Rubinstein decided America needed her. For, as she said, "I came in the winter. The women all used dead white powder; their lips were grey; their noses were red from cold." She swiftly put an end to that.

This shy Muray study of her was made shortly before her greatest business *coup*. In 1928 she sold out two-thirds of her business for $7,300,000. The new owners managed to run it into the ground even before the stock market crashed, and a year later Helena bought back control for $1,500,000 and late in 1929 married her Georgian prince. At one time she owned seven homes: two in France and one each in London, Mexico, Buenos Aires, New York and Greenwich, Connecticut. She used them as repositories for her great private art collection.

GEORGE HERMAN RUTH

I F you were sport-minded, you would have known the Twenties as the decade of Ruth. For it was between 1920 and 1931 that this singular individual dominated professional baseball as a member of the New York Yankees. It was in 1927 that Ruth accomplished the unprecedented feat of hitting 60 home runs in one major-league season, followed by 54 the next.

Since I was a sportswriter at the time, Babe Ruth loomed large in my life. I knew him personally, played handball with him during the winter months, traveled with him and wrote about him constantly.

But he also imposed himself thoroughly upon the national consciousness. He was a genuine American folk hero who had arrived via an orphanage and reform school to the eminence of being the highest-paid and best-known ballplayer of his time. He was also unique, and I cannot escape the feeling that only those times could have given rise to him and his enormous popularity and grip upon the public imagination.

His record has since been broken by Roger Maris, and yet Maris' accomplishment has fallen somehow into the so-what department and he himself is almost neglected.

There was the most overwhelming outpouring of love for the Babe. The boys of the country idolized him, and millions who had never even seen a baseball game followed his career.

We not only reported his activities in the ball yard, but wallowed emotionally in his personal life, his problems with gluttony and other vices which brought him into conflict with his team manager and fellow players. Once even the Mayor of New York, James J. Walker, made a tearful plea to the Babe to reform for the sake of the dirty-faced kids in the street. When he died of cancer on August 17, 1948, an entire nation mourned as though a king had passed away. Well, one had.

RUTH ST. DENIS
AND TED SHAWN

TED SHAWN, who a few years ago celebrated his golden wedding with Ruth St. Denis, was probably one of the most courageous young men in the United States. For one frozen January night in 1914 he dropped off a train in Gallup, New Mexico, proposing to give a dance recital garbed in a flame-colored chiton before an audience of sombreroed, gun-toting cowpokes. He did, too, and survived.

When Shawn was twenty-one and a pre-theology student at Denver University, he decided suddenly to abandon the ministry and become a dancer. An appalled fraternity brother made an impassioned plea, groaning, "But, Ted, *men* don't dance!"

And it was true—in the U.S. into which Ted Shawn was born in 1891. Men didn't dance, unless it was the vaudevillean buck-and-wing or soft-shoe. Yet by the end of the 1920's Ted Shawn and his partner and wife, Ruth St. Denis, had changed all that—had introduced, maintained and toured the first great American ballet and dance company, and had founded the Denishawn School, where every dance technique was taught and future greats were developed.

Ruth St. Denis, who began her career as a comparitively undistinguished vaudeville and musical-comedy dancer and actress for David Belasco, turned to Egypt and India and studied Hindu philosophy. She produced a ballet called *Radha* in 1906 and successfully toured Europe with it for three years. From the time of her marriage to Ted Shawn until today, she has never flagged in her devotion to classic and ancient Oriental dances. Between them they took the leers and the snide laughter out of creative dancing.

Muray noted Ruth St. Denis as one of the most exquisite creatures who ever faced his cameras.

TONY SARG

THIS Guatemalan-born son of a British Art Museum curator ought to be remembered by more people alive today than perhaps any other in this volume, for he worked his enchantment upon them when they were children. He was not only a puppeteer and a maker of marionettes, but he designed the famous three-story-high balloon figures that floated down Broadway in New York for the annual Thanksgiving Day parade of Macy's department store.

The establishment, the parades and the balloons were in those days a feature, just as a prior generation remembered Siegal and Cooper, which had a fountain in the lobby. Macy's window was famous for the curious ceremony in which, as a part of the vulgate language, we were often invited to participate.

Grotesque balloons aside, Tony Sarg had learned woodcarving from a German grandfather, and, working as a freelance artist in London, he rented the legendary original of Dickens' *Old Curiosity Shop*. He restored the room attributed to Little Nell and began making puppets, at the same time founding there his first puppet theater. In 1915 he moved to the United States and became a Greenwich Villager and an American citizen, presenting his first marionette shows at the Neighborhood Playhouse on Henry Street. From then on Tony Sarg's marionettes and Sarg himself were a part of the American scene, for he toured his animated wooden dolls all over the country.

That woodcarving German grandfather ran strongly in his veins, for even though Sarg was a successful commercial artist, his first love and concern was always children. The young of that decade were brought up on his picture books and the comical creatures with which he filled them. He designed toys and toy departments and Christmas window displays and was one of the first to produce animated cartoons, even before Disney.

ANDRÉS SEGOVIA

HE looks like a professor, but here is the world's most famous guitarist. Today, in his old age, Andrés Segovia must be driven out of his mind by the electrically amplified, ubiquitous plunking on the instrument he refined to concert performances of Bach, Haydn, Mendelssohn, De Falla and music especially composed for him by such as Villa-Lobos and Castelnuovo-Tedesco.

Born in Linares, Spain, in 1894, young Andrés turned to the guitar after preliminary struggles with the violoncello and the piano.

The guitar is one of the most ancient of instruments, for in all likelihood it is a descendant of the Roman cithara, which had come to Greece via Assyria and was brought to Spain by Roman colonizers. For all of its popularity in Spain, however, the guitar had little standing in spite of the fact that Paganini, the eccentric violinist, Boccherini and Berlioz were all guitarists or composed for it.

Segovia gave his first concert in Granada at the age of fourteen. It was received with indulgent smiles. He made his debut in Town Hall, New York, in 1928 before an audience of skeptics who remained to cheer him, and the event was described as "one of the most extraordinary and engrossing recitals of music that has ever taken place in a New York concert hall."

Do you like ghost stories? Segovia has one. When he was seventeen and broke, he went to Manuel Ramirez in Madrid, the Stradivarius of guitar makers, and begged to rent one of his creations. The master craftsman laughed at the idea, but handed him a fine one and said, "Try this. Let me hear you." Segovia played passionately. Ramirez presented it to him: "Take it with you through the world, and may your labors make it fruitful."

"I played it everywhere," Segovia narrates. "I loved it with all my heart. Years later, in Berlin' as I finished a recital there was a sharp noise. My guitar had cracked. The next day I received a wire Manuel Ramirez had died at the very moment the guitar's life had ended."

MARGARET SEVERN
AND W. T. BENDA

At the very beginning of the roaring Twenties, in the first of *The Greenwich Village Follies* which called attention to the mine of talent extant in New York's Little Bohemia, there occurred one of the most remarkable collaborations in the history of the theater of the dance.

An émigré Polish artist, Wladyslaw Theodor Benda, arrived in the United States in 1899 and became a popular illustrator for the magazines of the day. But more and more his hobby—creating bizarre and striking masks—took up his time, his energies and his interest.

In New York there was a most deliciously lovely creature, a twenty-year-old, European-trained, Alabama-born dancer by the name of Margaret Severn.

Miss Severn donned Mr. Benda's masks and danced in them, producing startling and weird transformations. The masks changed the dancer; the dancer brought the dead, stiff, papier-maché faces to life so that the painted expressions seemed to alter with the exquisite movements of her body, and our generation experienced a new thrill.

She danced in masks of tragedy, of horror, of silly doll-faces and of laughter, with stunning effect.

There was a curious affinity between the masks and the performer. Benda said, "Masks have more power than most persons imagine. See, I put on this one and immediately begin acting out what it represents."

To illustrate the point, he donned a mask of a comical old man with protruding eyebrows. The dignified Mr. Benda's personality changed into that of a clown, gay but pathetic in the same instant.

And now Margaret Severn: "A mask has a quality which is undeniably occult and it's a fact that each one seems to have its own personality to which the wearer is subservient. I never 'composed' these dances; I simply put on the mask and then *it* danced."

GEORGE BERNARD SHAW

AMONG the myriad reasons that led Frank Crowninshield to send Muray to photograph George Bernard Shaw at the age of seventy was that G.B.S. regularly spat in our eye. He habitually ridiculed and scoffed at Americans, and in spite of our admiration for him and the critical and financial success of his plays here, he obstinately and consistently refused all invitations to visit the United States.

Later, on a world tour with Mrs. Shaw in 1933, he made a stop in San Francisco, where curiosity drove him to visit the San Simeon ranch of William Randolph Hearst. From there he went to New York, where he remained for exactly twenty-six hours, during which time he delivered his only American lecture. He drew the largest audience ever to crowd into the Metropolitan Opera House, and they heard him advise the United States to scrap its constitution, nationalize its banks, destroy the power of financiers and cancel all war indebtedness.

One knew that Shaw was a Socialist, and Socialism was then as dirty a word as Communism is today. But Shaw became a peculiarly American pet, as evidenced by the success of the Theatre Guild production of *Saint Joan* in 1923. The same decade saw performances of *Heartbreak House* and *Back to Methuselah*.

In *Saint Joan*, as interpreted by St. John Ervine, the British authority on Shaw, the generation learned something of Shavian religious philosophy: namely, that the Life Force—God—is an imperfect power striving to become perfect, with all existence occupied in this struggle. Man, according to Shaw, is still on probation, but if we fail to achieve God's purpose, He will become impatient and scrap mankind as He scrapped the mammoth and other prehistoric beasts.

Today, almost two decades after Shaw's death at the age of ninety-four, if Shaw's guess is right, we must be high on the list for the next scrapping.

OTIS SKINNER

OUR decade saw many actors launched, but we also inherited renowned old-time mummers who had been around for so long and appeared so frequently upon the boards during this period that they seemed to belong to it exclusively. We saw Otis Skinner in *Blood and Sand* with his actress daughter, Cornelia; as *Sancho Panza;* in *The Merry Wives of Windsor;* as Papa Juan in *A Hundred Years Old;* and, in 1931, in a most moving performance when, after thirteen years' absence, Maude Adams returned to play Portia to his Shylock.

Yet other generations also called Otis Skinner their own, as when in 1911 he played the beggar Hajj in Edward Knoblock's famous Oriental play, *Kismet,* a performance which he repeated in both a silent and a sound film. During his lifetime Skinner played more than 325 parts, including 16 Shakespearean roles, and produced or directed at least 33 plays.

He reached back into the times of John Drew, Ada Rehan, May Irwin and Augustin Daly, in whose company he played in the 1880's. Ten years later he was a member of the troupe of Edwin Booth and leading man to Helena Modjeska.

Like so many who have gravitated to the theater, Otis Skinner, born in Cambridge, Massachusetts, in 1858, was the son of a clergyman. He started his career as a clerk in Hartford, Connecticut, by which time the Civil War was a thing of the past and modern America had begun to emerge.

His father took his decision to become a professional actor with commendable resignation. His mother pronounced her opinion in no uncertain terms: "Otis," she said, "you will never succeed. You can't even talk straight." Exactly half a century after this gloomy prophecy her son was awarded a medal by the American Academy for excellence in speech and diction.

He died in 1942 at the age of eighty-three. His legacy was his talent, which he bequeathed to his daughter, Cornelia Otis Skinner.

ALBERT SPALDING

ALBERT SPALDING was as American as the Fourth of July, Boston clam chowder or a baseball catcher's mitt. As a matter of fact, he came from the family that manufactured and marketed the latter, along with other sporting goods. For he was the son of J. Walter Spalding, co-founder of A. G. Spalding and Brothers. He was an officer in the United States Army in two world wars. He happened also to be a violin virtuoso. Albert was handsome enough to have been an actor and sufficiently talented as well to write a biographical novel.

When Spalding graduated from the Conservatory of Bologna at the age of fourteen, his family was told that he had passed his examination with the highest marks ever granted since a similar diploma had been given to Wolfgang Amadeus Mozart, over a hundred years previously.

He was born in Chicago in 1888, but when he was seven his family moved to Florence for the winter, and there young Albert became a violinist almost by accident. He had expressed a childish wish for a violin for Christmas. The family humored him by giving him what amounted to no more than a toy and cost in the neighborhood of $4. Within a year the boy was making this poor instrument sing, and then his studies began.

Albert Spalding was the great switch. While a plethora of Russian fiddlers and boy prodigies invaded the United States, he, the clean-cut American son of a manufacturer of golf balls, tennis rackets and boxing gloves, made his debut in Paris. When Spalding made his first U.S. appearance in 1908, at Carnegie Hall as soloist with the New York Symphony under Walter Damrosch, he occupied the unique position of an American-born artist with a European reputation.

Fighter as well as fiddler, he served in World War I as a lieutenant in the Army Aviation Corps and adjutant to the late Mayor Fiorello LaGuardia. In 1944 a certain "Major Sheridan" broadcast in Italian to the Italian resistance groups behind the German lines. Major Sheridan was the late Albert Spalding.

FRED STONE

THE training ground for the great knockabout, catch-as-catch-can, try-anything-once comedians, alas, is no more. The minstrel show is a thing of the past, the medicine men no longer criss-cross the country, the small circuses have been forced out of business, vaudeville is dead and the night-club circuit is about the only outlet where a young acrobat can make a living.

It was different in the day of Fred Stone, one of the most beloved and delightful of performers. Born in a log cabin back in 1874, he reached into the heart of the Twenties with such shows as *Jack o'Lantern*, *Tip-Top*, *Stepping Stones*, *Criss-Cross* and others, all produced at the Globe Theatre on Broadway. For eighteen years this was the only New York playhouse in which the comedian appeared.

When he was nine, Fred Stone started backyard tumbling and acrobatics with his brother. At thirteen he had already spent two seasons with a circus troupe, and thereafter it was a steady series of carnivals, medicine shows and minstrel troupes in which the boy learned every phase of knockabout comedy. He formed a vaudeville partnership with an ex-minstrel man, and the team of Montgomery and Stone was famous long before the 1920's.

Famous, too, was a book which had played a great part in my own childhood, *The Wizard of Oz*, by L. Frank Baum. Fred Stone created the role of the Scarecrow when it was made into a play, and he became an overnight sensation and the idol of children.

I seem to have grown up with Fred Stone and his wonderful shows, and part of the fun each time he appeared in a new extravaganza was to see what new specialty he had acquired. Always an agile, rubber-legged, acrobatic dancer, he turned up one year on ice skates, the next on a slack wire; then came roping with a Western lariat, knife-throwing, bareback riding and daring trapeze work. His home life was model and he was a crusader for clean plays. I wish he were still with us.

GLORIA SWANSON

IN 1957 at a Big Brothers luncheon at the Advertising Club in Washington, D.C., a tiny woman who described herself as a mother of three and a grandmother of six addressed an audience on the subject of malnutrition in the United States, its possible effect upon juvenile delinquency and the need for healthy nutrition to make healthy minds. Hers was the theory that malnutrition was the first cause of mental deficiency, and she orated:

"It is horrifying to know that 99 percent of our citizens are eating more than 276 chemicals (this was the figure in 1952, no doubt it's greater now) which have never been pretested for their chronic effect on human body and mind. I tremble to think what kind of minds and bodies my grandchildren's children will have if this continues."

Scientist? Schoolteacher? Not at all! Here is Grandma—Gloria Swanson, born Josephine May Swenson in 1899 to a captain of the United States Army Transport. She first graduated from a course of ducking custard pies with the Keystone Cops and then illuminated a series of bathing-beauty comedies with Mack Sennett. Thereafter she became one of the notable personalities of the silent motion pictures and an actress of stature who, as a performer, is still in demand today on stage, screen and television.

She not only played the lead in such films as *Bluebeard's Eighth Wife*, *Madame Sans-Gêne*, *Stage Struck*, *Prodigal Daughters* and the title role in *Sadie Thompson*, but has also been a producer, a dress designer and, in her later years, a passionate crusader for the purity of foods, the chief concern of her unprofessional life. At one time she was the Marquise de la Falaise de la Coudraye, and played that part, too, up to the hilt.

NORMA AND
CONSTANCE TALMADGE

*E*N *MEDAILLON* are two of the most fabled stars of the silent screen—Norma and Constance Talmadge, of whom, like the Gish sisters, one was a serious actress and the other a comedienne. In the case of the Talmadges there was a third sister, Natalie, who is better remembered as a wife of Buster Keaton.

All three girls were born in Brooklyn around the beginning of the Nineteen Hundreds, and brought considerable fame to Erasmus Hall High School by having attended it.

At the age of fourteen, Norma was registered by her mother at a more profitable institution of learning, namely the old Vitagraph Studio on Avenue W in Flatbush. Norma had what it took and soon began the same sensational rise that we have seen with the Gishes, Mary Pickford and others, except that as she climbed the ladder of success she had the good sense to marry the boss, Joseph M. Schenck. He, as president and producer, set up a producing unit for her.

And sister Connie came too. She had the talent, only she played it for laughs.

And if you would know what writing *about* movies was like in those days, here is an extract of an interview with Connie from the Brooklyn *Eagle*, dated July 3, 1921:

" 'My first role,' laughed Constance, 'was that of a lady's maid. I used to go to the studio with Norma in the early days and hook her up.'

"Connie looked very pretty and childish arrayed in crumpled gingham," burbled the interviewer. "It is a John Emerson–Anita Loos scenario. Just at this moment Mr. Emerson, who was directing the picture, appeared and told us something about it. It is a comedy and it will try to say that people should be allowed to do the things they want to do and are consequently best suited to do, since the Blue Laws would have things otherwise. We betray no confidence in saying that the story ends with the heroine marrying a rich man, played no doubt by Kenneth Harlan, who is much in evidence on the set."

THE THEATRE GUILD

THIS was the Theatre Guild in its early days. Standing are Philip Moeller, Lawrence Langner, Lee Simonson, Maurice Wertheim; seated, Helen Westley and Theresa Helburn.

Moeller was a playwright and stage director, Langner a patent lawyer, Simonson a designer, Wertheim a Wall Street banker and theater-lover. Helen Westley was an actress and Theresa Helburn a playwright. The purpose of their coming together was to establish a serious American theater which would not only foster our own young playwrights whose work was considered uncommercial by Broadway managers, but also present plays of European writers. This association was formed at the close of World War I. By 1924 it had succeeded beyond its most sanguine expectations.

Four of these colleagues had worked together in the Washington Square Players, founded in a Greenwich Village bookshop in the late winter of 1915: Moeller, Langner, Simonson and Miss Westley. And before they disbanded in the spring of 1917 because of the war, this collection of passionate lovers of the theater produced some fifty one-act plays by such authors as Maeterlinck, Andreyev, Chekov, Schnitzler, Musset and Wedekind.

The adjacent group was to prove during the roaring Twenties that an artistic success could be a box-office hit as well, for in 1924 they had two smash hits on Broadway—Molnár's *The Guardsman*, starring the Lunts, and Sidney Howard's *They Knew What They Wanted*. They had already presented Molnár's *Liliom*, Shaw's *Heartbreak House, Back to Methuselah, Saint Joan* and *The Devil's Disciple*, and Elmer Rice's *The Adding Machine*. Before the end of the decade they had produced Rodgers and Hart, DuBose and Dorothy Heyward, S. N. Behrman, Philip Barry and, above all, America's greatest playwright, Eugene O'Neill.

The mainsprings of this tremendous array of theatrical talent were the late Lawrence Langner, the lawyer with the nose for the theater; his wife, Armina Marshall; and the late, dynamic Terry Helburn, who gave up playwriting to become the director general of the group.

NICHOLAS MURAY
NEW YORK

JOHN CHARLES THOMAS

JOHN CHARLES THOMAS was the American baritone who triggered a revolt in one of the most unlikely places for the spirit of rebellion to raise its head, namely the Metropolitan Opera House. In 1932 the late Clarence Whitehill, a leading baritone at the Met, resigned in protest against the policy of the management of Giulio Gatti-Casazza in discriminating against American singers and in particular against Mr. Thomas. In 1933 John Charles Thomas made his debut with the Metropolitan and scored a triumphal success in *La Traviata*.

He was a whole man, was John Charles Thomas, an ex-U.S. Marine with a glorious voice, a powerful stage presence and a wholesome attitude toward life that made him one of the best-known and best-liked concert and operetta singers of the era.

A sampling of the clubs to which he belonged at the time of his death in 1960, at the age of sixty-eight, gives an idea of his extra-curricular interests and activities. They included five yacht clubs, the American Power Boat Association, the Artists and Writers Golf Association, the Dutch Treat, the Athletic Clubs of New York and Los Angeles, the Bath and Tennis at Palm Beach and the Sailfish Club of Florida.

And, of course, he was born a minister's son as well, which in our expanding American mythology was almost the equivalent of the Good Fairy appearing at birth at the cradleside.

At the age of ten he was already singing in the choir of the Methodist church at Meyersdale, Pennsylvania, where he was born. His family hoped that he would study for what was then known as "the cloth." John Charles opted for music, captured a scholarship at the Peabody Conservatory of Music and later went to Holland to train. From 1913 until the war, he became a musical-comedy star in such remembered shows as *Apple Blossoms* and *Maytime* and a series of Gilbert-and-Sullivan revivals with DeWolf Hopper, and a radio and concert artist through 1930.

In the end, the voice and the man were too big to be kept down.

CARL VAN VECHTEN AND FANIA MARINOFF

SOMEHOW the essence of Carl Van Vechten seems to be contained in an anecdote he told on himself in his reminiscences, recorded for the Columbia Oral History and quoted in Edward Lueders' book on Van Vechten. Born and raised in Cedar Rapids, Iowa in the 1880's, as a young boy he was sparking his girl on the steps of her front porch one hot summer's night and seeking to impress her.

Van Vechten recounts, "I said to her—'I'm so damned bored with this town. I'd like to put on a bath towel and run through the streets naked. I'd do anything to make some excitement.'"

There was a lot less Cedar Rapids in the young lady than in young Van Vechten. As he admits, "She didn't say a word. She just went into the house, came out with a bath towel and said, 'Go ahead, Carl.'"

He didn't then. But after 1907, when he migrated to New York via Chicago and fell in with Mabel Dodge and the Greenwich Village crowd, Carl Van Vechten figuratively went charging naked and towelless through a number of American myths and credos.

He had three definite careers: music critic, novelist and photographer, to which must be added arts enthusiast, collector, civil-rights exponent and discoverer of Black Harlem and the Negro intellectual life. He was also a noted cat-lover and the husband of a Russian Jewish actress, Fania Marinoff, who was constantly in work on the New York stage, and with whom he lived for more than half a century up to the time of his death at eighty-four in 1964.

Van Vechten was no rival to Muray with the camera, for portrait photography had been chiefly a hobby with him. When he turned to it full-time, he usually gave the copies away. I have a handful of prints he made of me at a time when, apparently, he was photographing *anyone* who would sit still for him. Later Carl was heard to say proudly, "I've photographed everybody from Matisse to Isamu Noguchi. My first subject was Anna May Wong, my second Eugene O'Neill." He also captured a real mixed bag—Theodore Dreiser, Gene Tunney, Joe Louis, William Faulkner, Salvador Dali, Aleck Woollcott and Gertrude Stein.

His novels of the Twenties, *Peter Whiffle*, *The Blind Bow-Boy*, *The Tattooed Countess*, *Red*, *Firecrackers* and *Nigger Heaven*, bit American pseudo-culture deeply in the ankle.

GANNA WALSKA

IF the delirious decade was famous for its celebrities—writers, artists, actors and divas who succeeded—it was equally so for some who did not. One of these was the Polish singer Mme. Ganna
Walska, who all through the postwar period fought a desperate, courageous and sometimes pathetic
battle to succeed as an operatic star. She had looks; she had determination; she had a series of
wealthy husbands, jewelry and beautiful clothes. But she didn't have the critics.

For the 1920's saw the rise of the reviewers and paid carpers. As the audience for all forms of
entertainment grew, so the reviewers' power waxed to the point where many of them, in their own
estimation, were little gods.

Of these, the most feared were the music critics, for the art they covered was such that not one
out of a hundred readers knew what they were talking about or was able to argue. If a commentator
on music disputed the tempi of a conductor or railed against his orchestral shadings, none but a
professional musician could say whether or not he was writing through his hat.

Equally, the pretensions of singers were not quite so simple to equate. The critics drew a bead on
Mme. Walska, and the running affray kept newspaper readers and music-lovers entertained for
years.

The story goes that when Ganna was twenty and living in Moscow, she fell in love with a handsome foreign attaché. In order to impress him, she took singing lessons. The love affair never developed, but the voice did. She made her New York debut with none other than Enrico Caruso, singing
the duet from Bizet's *Pearl Fishers* at one of the Biltmore Morning Musicales.

The most famous of her marriages was to Harold McCormick of the McCormick Reaper family,
and she appeared in a number of out-of-town opera companies. She seemed always to be with us,
but she never quite made it.

FANNIE WARD

PRACTICALLY every generation gives rise to some extraordinary woman who for a time produces the illusion of having discovered the fountain of youth. Just as Marlene Dietrich has dismissed age today, so Fannie Ward, a character in and out of the public prints as actress, divorcée and example of eternal youth, was one of the gayer enigmas of the Twenties. Her name entered the language, so that one used to say, "My God, So-and-so must be older than Fannie Ward!" And how old she actually was makes a nice little mystery even today, for it has never been solved.

When Muray made this study of her early in the Twenties, he said that she was sixty-four. But she looks thirty. She died in 1938, said to be nearly eighty. Give or take a year, that would make her birth date about 1859. Yet before she became famous as a youthful grandmother, she said she was born in 1875, which would have made her age at her death sixty-three. Later she put her birthday as 1872. Neither of these dates matches up with the photograph and what she apparently told Muray privately. But if she was born in 1859, sixty-four would bring her to the year 1923, about the time that Nick was photographing the great and the near great. How old, then, was Fannie?

In the Twenties she was known as a "peppy *young* flapper" with a skin as smooth and firm as that of an infant, and she liked to mystify reporters and interviewers as to how it was done. Her advice varied from "proper manipulation of muscles" to the use of a "Siberian snow face mask"— the secret of which, alas, is now lost—and finally, she announced that the best way for a woman to remain young was to marry a young husband, a preachment she practiced herself.

She played in film and stage roles almost to the day of her death.

FRED WARING

WE all danced as though we had been stung by an army of tarantulas through those light-hearted, gin-soaked Twenties. Someone had to make the music. Fred Waring and his Pennsylvanians were the favorite band to which we Shagged, Charlestoned and Black-Bottomed.

Waring's was the "sound" of the decade. His was the highest-paid and most popular orchestra, and there are many who will tell you that, as music to listen to and move by, it hasn't been improved upon since.

It all started when the century was young, with four high-school kids in the town of Tyrone, Pennsylvania, putting together a combo they called the Scrapiron Quartette. Fred Waring and Fred Buck plucked banjos; Fred's brother Tom was at the piano; and the drums were beaten by an odd, frog-voiced character by the name of Poley McClintock, a natural comic.

Waring's grandfather had founded Penn State College. The four boys went there. Fred wanted to be an architect. When this quartet tried out for the Penn State glee and dramatic clubs, they all failed miserably. To console themselves, they went back to their old combo, only now it was called the Waring-McClintock Snap Orchestra and played dates for $60 a night. When the dancers kept stopping to watch Poley, the four knew they had something.

In 1921, when invited to play for the overflow crowd at the University of Michigan Jay Hop, they renamed themselves Waring's Pennsylvanians and stole the show from two nationally known orchestras.

They made their initial radio broadcast over WWJ in Detroit and from then on were practically never off the air. The band, augmented and led by Fred, was held over for fourteen weeks at the Balaban and Katz Theatre in Chicago.

They captured Paris at Les Ambassadeurs, where Marie Dressler, Garbo, Pola Negri, Prince George of Greece and Ambassador Herrick used to come to hear them play.

Abrupt Change of Subject Department: You must at some time have used a Waring Mixer or Blendor in your kitchen. No bar or household is without one. Inventor and adapter, manufacturer and marketeer: Fred Waring.

CLIFTON WEBB

WE have seen characters from Nickolas Muray's album move from the choir loft, vaudeville and musical-comedy stage into grand opera. The late Clifton Webb started at the top, singing in *Mignon* at the Back Bay Opera House in Boston in December 1911, and descended happily from this eminence into a musical-comedy actor, song-and-dance man, ballroom dancer and teacher, and stiff-upper-lipped British-type comedian in moving pictures.

Everyone thought that Webb was English, due to the slender, handsomely chiseled face with the Guard's mustache, the impeccable diction and the elegant taste in clothes. As a matter of fact, he was born in the Midwest.

When he switched from opera to operetta, his ability as a dancer attracted so much attention that he teamed up with various partners—Bonnie Glass, Mae Murray and Jennie Dolly (half of a pair of a famous sister act Jennie and Rosie Dolly, a couple of kids from Budapest whose presence in vaudeville likewise brightened our days).

On the side, he opened a dance studio which was the only rival to that of the team of Vernon and Irene Castle.

Paris knew him too. Elsa Maxwell and Captain Edward Molyneux opened a night club there, and Clifton Webb and Jennie Dolly were the stars. It was a ball. Molyneux did Jennie's clothes—a different frock every night. At the opening, Jennie made her entrance wearing 150 birds of paradise in her hair and over her dress a cloth-of-gold cloak with fresh gardenias pinned all over the front. Webb followed with two turbaned blackamoor boys carrying baskets of corsages. Walking among the tables, Clifton handed his corsages to the ladies, while Jennie attached a gardenia to the lapel of each man. Then the two danced on a black velvet carpet. And very few suspected that the exquisite male dancing partner was a kid from Indianapolis.

This generation remembers him as the baby-sitter Mr. Belvedere, who in the film *Sitting Pretty* satisfied every father who ever saw it when Webb dumped a bowl of oatmeal over the head of a small, sweet child.

JOHNNY WEISSMULLER

JOHNNY WEISSMULLER was a swimmer, but not just *a* swimmer: he was *the* swimmer, the champion of champions at his sport in the golden decade of athletes who became national idols.

A young Adonis, handsome, cast in the mold of the idealized American (although he happened to be of German extraction), Weismuller dramatized swimming during those ten years by holding every free-style record from the 100-yard to the half-mile. He swam on two American Olympic teams (1924 and 1928), won five gold medals and, every time he entered the tank wearing the U.S. Olympic shield on his swim suit, broke a world record. It was a common phrase to remark that such-and-such an athlete was unbeatable, but Weissmuller actually fulfilled it. From 1921 to 1929 he never lost a free-style race.

It was not enough just to be a winner. There had to be the personality that went with it, that intangible which we called star quality. Weissmuller had it. He was in his own way an artist who happened to use the technique of swimming to express himself.

And, like so many of the characters in this volume, Weissmuller had a dual career. Just as the decade came to an end, Metro-Goldwyn-Mayer was looking for an actor to play the part of Tarzan, a wild boy grown up in a jungle, swinging from tree to tree, a character invented by a best-selling pulp writer Edgar Rice Burroughs. They stripped Weissmuller to his magnificent buff. He stood six foot three and a third inches, with wide shoulders, flat belly, no hips or buttocks and marvelously muscled legs. For the next twelve years Weissmuller, swinging from studio tree to studio tree, was one of the best-known moving-picture actors in the world.

H. G. WELLS

IT was the fate of H. G. Wells, novelist, historian and one of the leaders of socialist thought in Great Britain for many years, to be known to us in the Twenties more for his science fiction than for his two most important books, *The Outline of History*, published in 1920, and *A Short History of the World*, in 1922.

To us, Wells was the man who had written the most exciting stories of our adolescence, such as *The Time Machine, The Island of Dr. Moreau, The Invisible Man, The War of the Worlds, When the Sleeper Wakes* and *Tales of Space and Time*, all of which had appeared before the year 1900. What stuff this was—Martians and ray guns, invisibility and imagining oneself going backward or forward in time. I remember making my own discovery of H. G. Wells in the public library and being hardly able to believe that such a famous writer, and an Englishman to boot, could have turned out such marvelous yarns.

For to the intellectuals he was the novelist of *Kipps: The Story of a Simple Soul, The History of Mr. Polly, Tono-Bungay, The New Machiavelli* and *Mr. Britling Sees It Through*.

This man who for all readers was a modern Jules Verne and a prophet died in 1946, long before the first human had been launched into space. In 1938 Orson Welles terrified the nation and caused a wave of mass hysteria the night of October 30 with a broadcast radio drama that led thousands to believe that men from Mars had invaded the Earth and were spreading death and destruction throughout New York and New Jersey. What Orson had done was to rewrite Wells's *The War of the Worlds* into a radio drama with sound effects and pseudo news-agency reports. H. G. denounced this as an outrage.

Born in 1866, he was still living when the atomic bomb that he had prophesied in a novel in 1914 was dropped upon Hiroshima in 1945.

MRS. HARRY PAYNE WHITNEY

OUR press was prodigal with great stories. Newspaper columns today are equally replete with eye-poppers, thrillers and oddities, but ours were more simple ones. They were cast in the mold of the still-emerging American fairytale: the struggling journalist from the Midwest whose play was a sensational hit on Broadway, or the child, born practically in a theatrical trunk to poor vaudevilleans, who became a great star. Our favorite, of course, was the "from rags to riches" theme. But we were equally fascinated with a switch when it took place. Gertrude Vanderbilt Whitney made it the other way around.

She was a girl who started at the top of the social swing, made her way down to the slums of Greenwich Village and succeeded in becoming one of the outstanding American sculptresses.

To make this early picture of the young artist at work, Muray had to lug his portrait camera and tripod only half a block or so through Greenwich Village from his own studio to the remodeled stable at No. 19 MacDougal Alley where the heiress was putting in her twelve or fourteen hours a day.

Gertrude Vanderbilt married Harry Payne Whitney in 1896. Her Dun and Bradstreet rating was circa $200,000,000. She was then nineteen and a year later began to devote herself to the study of art. In Paris she lived in the art students' quarter and was a pupil of Andrew O'Connor and Auguste Rodin. After she set up her Village studio, she became a fully fledged, mature professional whose statues, groups and figures decorate Washington, New York and San Francisco.

She died in 1942 and is remembered not only for her own personal triumph, but because at all times during her early days she was ready to extend a financial helping hand to fellow artists.

LOUIS WOLHEIM

LOUIS WOLHEIM, actor, who died in 1933, simultaneously supported two cherished myths: that villainy is connected with physiognomy—evil men have evil faces—and that men who *played* the bad guys on stage and screen were in private life kindly gentlemen with tender hearts who wouldn't hurt a fly.

While Louis had been known to inflict bodily harm on barroom pests from time to time, he otherwise fitted the description, for in private life he was a philosopher, a wit, an admirer of Count Tolstoy, a linguist, mathematician and engineer. On stage he was Captain Flagg in *What Price Glory* and Yank Smith the stoker in Eugene O'Neill's shocker play *The Hairy Ape.*

Wolheim's face with its squashed-in nose was his fortune. And though born on the Jewish East Side in the 1880's, he didn't get it brawling or street fighting, but as Wolly Wolheim, Cornell full-back, 1905–1906. Wolheim, who had graduated from City College and was studying mechanical engineering at Cornell, recalled that his function on a football team was to act as a battering ram. During the course of this exercise, his nose was broken three times and eventually assumed the shape of guaranteed villainy, although after graduation he did nothing more heinous than cramming mathematics into young minds for six years at Cornell Preparatory School.

But the Twenties were waiting for him, for in 1918 he met Lionel Barrymore, who told him succinctly, "Anyone with a mug like yours should use it; it would be your fortune." Wolheim was impressed and made his debut with Lionel and John Barrymore in *The Jest*. His next role was in *The Hairy Ape*, in which he succeeded not only in terrifying the audience, but also in frightening the wits out of the actress Mary Blair, who played opposite him in the boiler-room scene. In Hollywood he played a succession of tough guys, mugs and gangsters and, in 1927, made headlines by proposing to have his nose redone by plastic surgery. His studio took out an injunction to prevent him from spoiling his lovely and commercial face.

ELINOR WYLIE

OUR era had its famous poetesses and they were remarkable women as well. Between 1921 and 1928 the principal poetic works of Elinor Wylie were *Nets to Catch the Wind, Black Armour, Trivial Breath* and *Angels and Earthly Creatures*. In prose she wrote *Jennifer Lorn, The Venetian Glass Nephew, The Orphan Angel* and *Mr. Hodge and Mr. Hazard*. Strange stories; sensitive, feverish poems; strange, sensitive feverish woman who died in 1928, the night after she had completed revisions on *Angels and Earthly Creatures*.

She was beautiful but also high-strung, frail and almost childishly vain of her loveliness.

She wrote poetry from 1921, but her life prior to this (she was born in 1885) was an astonishing story.

The daughter of a onetime Solicitor General of the United States, she was a Philadelphia Main Liner, carefully schooled, including a season in Paris and London with her sister Nancy Hoyt, the novelist. When she was twenty, she married Philip Hichborn, son of a Rear Admiral. In 1910 she startled Philadelphia society by eloping with Horace Wylie, a married man and fifteen years older. They lived abroad for five years as Mr. and Mrs. Waring.

Hichborn, her first husband, killed himself in 1912. Three years later the "Warings" returned to the United States, where, Wylie's wife having finally divorced him, they were able to marry.

The couple tried to live in Washington, but in those still straight-laced days Elinor's flouting of propriety was too much for the wives' union of Old Washingtonians and they were read out of the party. They moved to New York, where all the turmoil that had filled Elinor Wylie began to appear as poems. Yet her life problems were not yet done. In 1921 she divorced Horace Wylie, and two years later like at last met and married like when she wed William Rose Benét, poet and editor. From then until she died, the music of her words flowed uninterruptedly.

LORETTA YOUNG, POLLY ANN YOUNG AND SALLY BLANE

YOU would find it hard to make a choice among these three lovely dollies—Loretta, Sally Blane and Polly Ann, the three Young sisters. But Fate and Mervyn LeRoy determined that it was Loretta, the youngest, who would become one of the featured players of the Twenties.

She made her first film appearance at the age of four, when she was carried onto the set in a picture starring the perennial Fannie Ward. She was educated at a convent in Los Angeles, studied dancing under Ruth St. Denis and had to complete her education under the guidance of tutors because she was yet so very young when in 1927, quite by accident, she had her chance.

Mervyn LeRoy, who was directing for First National, telephoned to the home of the Youngs. He wanted Polly Ann for a part in a picture with Colleen Moore. But Polly Ann was out of town. The phone was answered by her brother Jack, a bright boy, who said, "Polly Ann is away, but we've got Loretta here. She looks an awful lot like her sister." The kid was fourteen.

"Send her out," ordered LeRoy. Colleen liked her, with the result that Loretta played her first role in Colleen's hit *Naughty But Nice*.

The following year a circus girl was wanted to play an equestrienne with the late Lon Chaney in the screen version of Andreyev's *He Who Gets Slapped*, which, naturally, was retitled *Laugh, Clown, Laugh*. Her training at the Denishawn School stood her in good stead and MGM selected her out of fifty candidates to play the lead.

Her real break was, of course, working with Chaney, who as one of the great character actors of the screen was an integral part of the Twenties, during which he was known as "The Man of a Thousand Faces." A real old pro, he taught the fifteen-year-old girl every trick of the trade. Sally and Polly Ann became actresses too, but it was the name of Loretta that was pinned to the firmament.

BLANCHE YURKA

THE only rival that Ruth Draper ever acknowledged in the field of the one-woman show was Blanche Yurka. And at that there was never any genuine comparison, for Miss Yurka confined herself to an evening of renditions of scenes from great plays in which she had starred in the Twenties, presenting a night of Aristophanes, Shakespeare, Molière, Sheridan, Congreve and Maxwell Anderson.

She was a gamut-runner who could span the distance between the tragic queen of John Barrymore's *Hamlet* or Lady Macbeth and the comedy of *Lysistrata*.

She was of the genre of the great ladies of the theater who made the stage thrilling and outstanding, particularly with her performance in Ibsen's *Wild Duck*.

And in connection with this play, Miss Yurka has a story to tell: While she was appearing in it and sat for this portrait, Nick gave in to her pleading request to have a fencing lesson.

She writes: "I had been lunging and parrying for about ten minutes when Nick said, 'I think that's enough for your first time.'

"I said, 'Nonsense' and insisted on continuing. Nick gave me that strange look from beneath his eyebrows and let me have my way. That night in *The Wild Duck*, as I sat in my chair in the opening scene, I realized that when my cue came for me to get up, I wasn't going to be able to do so. It took some quick thinking on my part to rearrange the business of the play for the next few minutes, I assure you! But all the time I could only think of Nick laughing if he could have seen me."

A thorough professional, on one of her few forays into films she made as great a success as in her stage appearances when she played Mme. Defarge in *A Tale of Two Cities*.

In 1965 she was presented with the Anniversary Award of the American National Theater and Academy.

DR. GREGORY ZILBOORG

GREGORY ZILBOORG, late noted psychiatrist, teacher, lecturer and specialist on suicide, fled from the Russian Bolshevik dictatorship in 1919 and came to the United States. While studying at Columbia University College of Physicians and Surgeons so that he could acquire an American medical license, he supported himself by, among other things, translating for the theater.

One of the plays he did was Andreyev's *He Who Gets Slapped* for the Theatre Guild. Lawrence Langner remembered how Zilboorg spent hours during rehearsals with the famous actor Richard Bennett (father of Constance and Joan), who was to play He.

"Lawrence," said the actor with a troubled expression on his handsome face, "this highbrow fellow Zilboorg keeps talking about this character's psychology and I simply don't know where the hell I'm at. Now tell me, is this a Bassanio part or a Mercutio part?"

Langner, feeling one thing was as safe to say as another, told him that it was a Mercutio part, and, satisfied that he had the "word," Bennett played him that way. In his delightful book *The Magic Curtain* Langner wrote with a straight face, "I feel sure it was Richard Bennett's failure to understand the character which . . . made our first production of the play so great a success."

Dr. Gregory Zilboorg was one of the first outriders of the eventual swarm of psychiatrists that was to turn up in America, and soon, like Bennett, none of us any longer knew where we were at. Before then we didn't know that we were neurotic, sick or psychotic; we were just crazy-happy, irresponsible and enjoying life. We didn't know what our old man had done to us as children, or that we had hated our mothers. All this was to change, as more and more we learned about the horrors that went on in our subconscious and what chancy creatures we were, at the mercy of that unquenchable impulse, sex. And by the late Fifties, when Dr. Zilboorg was gathered to his Russian ancestors, no one who could not casually drop a remark about "my analyst" could be considered "in."

INDEX

NICKOLAS MURAY

Nickolas Muray was born in Hungary in 1892. At the age of twelve he began his study of photography, photo-engraving and lithography, and at the end of his apprenticeship in Budapest he received an International Engraver's Certificate. In Berlin he perfected himself in advanced color photo-engraving, and in 1913 he came to New York, where he made color separations and halftone negatives for the Condé Nast Company and learned English in night school. In 1920 he opened a studio in Greenwich Village as a portrait photographer, and soon his photographs were appearing in the gravure section of the *New York Tribune*. During the 1920's his celebrity portraits in *Harper's Bazaar* and *Vanity Fair* made a celebrity of Muray himself. Later his increasing interest in color photography led to contracts with *Ladies' Home Journal* and *McCall's* for covers and fashion illustrations, and to innumerable advertising assignments. He died in 1965.

PAUL GALLICO

Paul Gallico was born in New York City in 1897 and grew up in New York to play football in high school and to captain his eight-oar crew at Columbia University. A gunner's mate in the U.S.N.R.F. in World War I, he became one of the highest-paid sports columnists and Sports Editor of the New York *Daily News*. After fourteen years of reporting on the activities of the great athletes of the time, he resigned in 1936 to write fiction, and soon his stories were appearing in *Saturday Evening Post*, *Cosmopolitan*, *Collier's*, *Redbook* and other magazines. During World War II he interrupted his freelance writing to become a war correspondent for *Cosmopolitan*. Among his most popular books are *The Snow Goose*, *The Small Miracle*, *Mrs. 'Arris Goes to Paris* and three classic animal tales—*The Abandoned*, *Thomasina* and *The Silent Miaow*. He has resided in Italy, Liechtenstein and Switzerland and now lives in the principality of Monaco.